"Words matter during a crisis. Th
hostage negotiators, emergen
professionals. Through extensive re
provide a fresh concept of con
emergency calls and it provides tools t

when a life is on the line.

—**C. Blair Sutherland**, *Ret. Director of Telecommunications and 911 Commission member, Massachusetts State Police, USA*

"This book will save lives! After seventeen years of crisis and hostage negotiation I thought I knew what I was doing... How I wish this had been available when I started out. It tells me what I should have been saying and where, by chance, I stumbled on just the right words I know why they worked. If people or lives depend on you, then this is the book for you."

—**Chula Rupasinha**, *Former UK Hostage Negotiator, UK*

"Finally! A book devoted to the "art" of emergency call taking, the authors take an in-depth analysis of the technical and subjective aspects of a call for help and teach us to communicate better for the person in crisis. This book should be on any must-read list for every emergency telecommunicator, supervisor, and executive worldwide."

—**Rich Lindfors**, *NRP, EMD Quality Improvement Manager, Richmond Ambulance Authority, Richmond, VA, USA*

"This book explores how police crisis negotiators and emergency dispatchers talk and interact in life-or-death situations. The reader is presented with real-life examples of distressing and emotional situations where lives are at stake and where every moment, word and turn of talk counts. With the detailed yet accessible analyses, the book is a compelling example of using conversation analysis to analyse real-time talk and interaction with an aim to develop and improve professional practices. It shows how formulating and delivering words in this or that way can lead to different outcomes; choosing and formulating the words correctly solves crisis situations and saves lives. The book provides practical and useful advice on how to interact in high stakes situations. The book is an excellent read for professionals who encounter people in crisis situations (e.g., police hostage and crisis negotiator and emergency dispatchers). It is also a fascinating read for academics who are interested in talk, language, grammar and social interaction. More generally, the book may find readers in people interested in crisis communication and the work of crisis professionals."

—**Pentti Haddington**, *Professor of English language and interaction, University of Oulu, Finland*

"This book manages to identify, quantify and put into words the practical skills of an experienced negotiator in a way that has never been done before. Their contributions have been integral in shaping and developing the language and tactics for overcoming resistance in particular, taught and deployed operationally by students and experienced negotiators alike. I would recommend anyone who wants to truly understand influential language through the eyes, ears and mouth of a negotiator to read this book."

—**Inspector Laura Burns**, *Training Lead, Hostage and Crisis Negotiator Unit, Police Scotland (2017–2020), Scotland*

Crisis Talk

Based on extensive analysis of real-time, authentic crisis encounters collected in the UK and US, *Crisis Talk: Negotiating with Individuals in Crisis* sheds light on the relatively hidden world of communication between people in crisis and the professionals whose job it is to help them.

The crisis situations explored in this book involve police hostage and crisis negotiators and emergency dispatchers interacting with individuals in crisis who threaten suicide or self-harm. The practitioners face various communicative challenges in these encounters, including managing strong emotions, resistance, hostility, and unresponsiveness. Using conversation analysis, *Crisis Talk* presents evidence of how practitioners deal with the interactional challenge of negotiating with people in crisis and how what they say shapes outcomes. Each chapter includes recommendations based on the detailed analysis of numerous cases of actual negotiation.

Crisis Talk shows readers how every turn taken by negotiators can exacerbate or solve the communicative challenges created by crisis situations, making it a unique and invaluable text for academics in psychology, sociology, linguistic sciences, and related fields, as well as for practitioners engaging in crisis negotiation training or fieldwork.

Rein Ove Sikveland is an Associate Professor at the Centre for Academic and Professional Communication at NTNU, Norway. His expertise is in conversation analysis and phonetics. Rein researches the linguistic and interactional practices that underpin practitioners' management of conversations in education, health services and crisis negotiations.

Heidi Kevoe-Feldman is an Associate Professor in the Department of Communication Studies at Northeastern University, USA. She uses conversation analysis to examine communication patterns and problems that arise in institutional settings. Recent research projects include working with emergency medical dispatch call centres with a focus on identifying various barriers (e.g. physical, psychological, and communication) that interfere with helping callers in a time of crisis.

Elizabeth Stokoe is Professor of Social Interaction in the Discourse and Rhetoric Group at Loughborough University, UK. Her current research interests are in conversation analysis, membership categorization, and social interaction in various ordinary and institutional settings, including neighbour mediation, police interrogation, role-play, and simulated interaction.

Crisis Talk

Negotiating with Individuals in Crisis

Rein Ove Sikveland
Heidi Kevoe-Feldman
Elizabeth Stokoe

Routledge
Taylor & Francis Group

LONDON AND NEW YORK

First published 2022
by Routledge
2 Park Square, Milton Park, Abingdon, Oxon OX14 4RN

and by Routledge
605 Third Avenue, New York, NY 10158

Routledge is an imprint of the Taylor & Francis Group, an informa business

© 2022 Rein Ove Sikveland, Heidi Kevoe-Feldman, and Elizabeth Stokoe

British Library Cataloguing-in-Publication Data
A catalogue record for this book is available from the British Library

Library of Congress Cataloging-in-Publication Data
A catalog record has been requested for this book

ISBN: 978-0-367-37531-7 (hbk)
ISBN: 978-0-367-37529-4 (pbk)
ISBN: 978-0-429-35489-2 (ebk)

DOI: 10.4324/9780429354892

Typeset in Calvert
by codeMantra

Contents

Acknowledgments

We express our deepest gratitude to the crisis negotiators, emergency dispatchers, and trainers for being calm and compassionate voices for those who want to end their life. Professionals have tremendous skill in working with anxious, terrified, and often angry people in crisis, walking them through the interactional steps to choose life. Crisis negotiators and emergency dispatchers save lives and it has been our privilege to analyse their expertise and experience.

This book would not have been possible without being granted access to the recordings of crisis negotiations and emergency calls that constitute its research material. We are grateful to the police officers in the UK, including some of the world's most experienced negotiators, who decided to become early adopters of conversation analytic research and took the rare step of releasing negotiation tapes. Similarly, we want to thank supervisors and coordinators at the emergency call center in the USA. As part of our research, we were also invited to participate in and observe hostage and crisis negotiation training, which became an invaluable part of our journey.

We would also like to thank Loughborough University's Institute of Advanced Studies and Northeastern University for, respectively, sponsoring Heidi Kevoe-Feldman's visiting fellowship and funding travel so that we could write together. Finally, we are grateful to the wonderful wider conversation analytic community, many of whom joined us at data sessions around the world, and reviewed our journal articles, helping us to consolidate the valuable analytic insights we present in this book.

Crisis talk, from practice to training

Chapter 1

DOI: 10.4324/9780429354892-1

WHAT IS THIS BOOK ABOUT?

This book sheds light on the relatively hidden world of real-time, as-it-happens, communication between people in crisis and the professionals whose job it is to help them. Based on extensive analysis of actual, authentic encounters collected in the UK and USA, the book aims to change how both academics and professionals research and practise communication in crisis situations.

Rather than aiming to produce a new model of crisis talk, or evaluate existing models (e.g., the 'Behavioural Change Staircase Model'; 'Behavioural Influence Staircase Model', see Ireland & Vecchi, 2009), we start with practice itself. From our analysis of what practitioners actually do, we build out and up from what works. While much is written about crisis communication – particularly in negotiation contexts – there is a general under-specification both of how models are implemented in real practice, and whether real practice matches up to the recognizable phases, procedures, and terms of the models.

The book will, therefore, *specify* but also *challenge* what we think we know about effective crisis communication and its component practices. While concepts such as 'rapport', 'active listening', or 'empathy' litter the models and guidance for crisis communication – as well as across professional practice of all kinds from medicine to commercial encounters – we will show that they are hard to pin down in actual social interaction. Instead, we will turn our analysis of the tacit expertise of practitioners into clear and research-based recommendations, offering an alternative approach grounded in evidence rather than on what we think works, or what works in simulations and role-play.

WHY ARE WE WRITING THIS BOOK?

We report on two bodies of research in the book: studies of *in situ* recordings of police negotiators interacting with suicidal persons in crisis in the UK, and of emergency service telephone dispatchers in the USA, including interactions with suicidal callers. Ever since the start of our collaboration, we noticed that many of the same practices were (in)effective in both settings, and in both countries. We therefore took the opportunity to incorporate our findings into existing training for negotiators and emergency dispatchers in the UK and the USA. Our focus was on identifying what 'expert' and 'experience' looks like in actual interaction. As this book will show, while many practitioners *do* what works, they do not *know* – on reflection, *post-hoc* – what they *actually did* that worked. Whether or not people have access to 'higher order cognitive processes' such as intentions, memories, and so on, and thus are able to answer questions such as "How did you solve this problem?" (e.g., in daily life, in the training room, or to a researcher), has been the subject of a vast trajectory of psychological science since the classic article on verbal reports of mental processes by Nisbett and Wilson (1977, p. 231). They argued that people have

> little or no direct introspective access to higher order cognitive processes. Subjects are sometimes (a) unaware of the existence of a stimulus that importantly influenced a response, (b) unaware of the existence of the response, and (c) unaware that the stimulus has affected the response. It is proposed that when people attempt to report on their cognitive processes, that is, on the processes mediating the effects of a stimulus on a response, they do not do so on the basis of any true introspection. Instead, their reports are based on a priori, implicit causal theories, or judgments about the extent to which a particular stimulus is a plausible cause of a given response.

As this book will show, the communicative practices that are effective in crisis talk are – if not the opposite of what models propose – sometimes counter-intuitive. For example, we will show how challenging persons in crisis can be productive but is advised against in existing models and guidance. In training environments, both trainers and trainees alike are accountable to written guidance and often train using role-play or simulation. As we have shown elsewhere (Stokoe, 2013; 2014; Stokoe & Sikveland, 2017; Stokoe et al., 2020), what happens in simulated interaction may contrast sharply with the actual practice it seeks to mimic. So, there is something of a vicious circle in models-training-guidance:

- When asked what they do that works, trainees are unable to recall their practice (negotiations might be hours long) at the level of accuracy and detail required.
- When reflecting on or reporting what they did to trainers (who may be senior members of the organization, and who get to decide whether trainees pass or fail courses), trainees are likely to report what they *think they ought to say* – that is, what is 'in the guidance', even if they think they did something different.
- When using role-play to train, both trainees and simulated interlocutors (those playing the role of person in crisis) act in ways that afford or constrain what we think we know about best practice.

Our research-based training replaces this vicious circle with a virtuous one that moves from practice to training and back to practice. Feedback has been positive:

> The team's inputs have been easily transferable, easily understood, and very quickly embedded into practical operations and in the training. It has had a specific impact on negotiations from the opening gambit and throughout the dialogue, be it verbal or even through text or email messages. Very small subtleties, or things that appear to be very small subtleties, have a significant impact.
>
> (Police training lead, UK)

Because our research starts with what happens on the ground, we have also been able to examine and develop training around topics that are not covered in existing research or training. As we will see in Chapter 7, a key part of crisis communication is the role of other professional parties in the ongoing interaction. For instance, police crisis negotiators work in teams, in which a secondary negotiator (the 'number two') is mandated to support the primary negotiator (who actually talks to the person in crisis) from behind the scenes. While the secondary negotiator can be influential in what happens, their role is almost completely missing in research and training:

> One of the most useful findings was about the role of the number two, because we'd never really broken that down, and considered not just what number two might say to number one, but whether they should actually be saying it. This has genuinely changed the way we work. I was number two a week ago and I was consciously aware, does the number one actually need to know this right now? Can it wait? When do we feed this in? So, the research has changed our practice and the practice of the cadre.
>
> (Police training lead, UK)

Therefore, we write this book to both academics and practitioners.

HOW IS THE BOOK STRUCTURED?

The book is structured across eight chapters. Chapters 2 to 6 map out the chronological development of crisis encounters from beginning to end, starting with their opening moments and ending with a person in crisis choosing to stay alive, and/or the emergency event concluding safely. We believe that readers will benefit from a structure that replicates real scenarios by bringing them through the various interactional challenges and opportunities that arise throughout these encounters. Recurrent features of crisis talk such as resistance, explicit orientations to agency and control, and hysteria, are pervasive throughout these encounters and are discussed in more detail throughout chapters. Each chapter presents data from the real encounters that demonstrate practices that work across different interactional settings, and each concludes with a box of takeaway practical strategies for professionals, tied to the chapter's empirical findings.

In this chapter, we start by diving straight into some brief examples of what crisis talk looks like; the challenges faced by practitioners, and the sorts of things we have found by closely scrutinizing the data. Next, we explain how we know what works; that is, how we make a case for identifying effective practice and recommending it as such. After a brief overview of existing literature on crisis talk, we move into a section that lays the groundwork for how to read and use the book. We will explain what our method of analysis – conversation analysis – is; how we collected the data and use it ethically; why we use a detailed transcript, and how to read the technical transcripts.

We hope that readers will be able to follow the narrative of the whole book, but also recommend, if pressed for time, starting with this chapter and the final one, in which we present a summary of all of the best practice we have identified.

THE CHALLENGE OF INTERACTING WITH A PERSON IN CRISIS

Many journeys start with a challenge. In this section, we introduce the challenge of interacting with persons in crisis through some brief illustrative examples. At the same time as introducing some of the central topics of the book, these examples introduce the reader to the basic format in which the data are presented. For the first few cases, we have simplified the transcript, but will present and explain further technical components later in the chapter.

A core challenge across all of our data is that, in crisis talk, the person in crisis typically resists, and sometimes rejects in strong and unconditional terms, the encounter itself – even if they have called 911 or stood on a building in such a way that members of the public can see them and read their likely intention. By definition, a 'negotiation' involves resistance and an extended interaction over an enduring series of turns (the utterances with which we build a conversation). Dispatchers and negotiators do not simply say "please come down" and get agreement in response. The fact that persons in crisis resist or reject the crisis conversation itself is, however, key to understanding what works in such encounters. For instance, in Example 1.1, a negotiator ('N') is trying to re-establish a conversation with a person in crisis ('PiC'), anonymized as "Mosi". Prior to this encounter, PiC prematurely ended a mobile phone conversation with the negotiators, and the negotiator is now addressing him from the ground in front of the building.

```
Example 1.1: Crisis negotiation (simplified
transcript)
01   N:    Mosi?
02              (pause)
03   N:    Mosi?
04              (pause)
05   N:    Mosi.
06              (pause)
07   N:    Is-
08              (long pause)
09   N:    What- what's your name.
10              (pause)
11   N:    What do you want me to call you.
12              (long pause)
```

The negotiator makes six attempts to get the person in crisis to engage in a conversation. The first three attempts involve calling Mosi's name, and then apparently asking him what his name is, or what, if not Mosi, he should call the person in crisis. The fact that the person in crisis takes no speaking turns in this example underlines the very basic challenge that negotiators face; yet, Mosi is not jumping. So, there are opportunities to be taken by the negotiator.

Also fundamental to how people in crisis respond throughout much of the negotiations are notions of personal agency, rationality, and control, as we will see in later chapters. This includes understanding and working with the fact that a person in crisis has made, in their own terms, a rational decision to end their life. While the tacit goal of a crisis encounter is to get the person in crisis to stay alive, they typically resist agreeing with the negotiator or dispatcher to do so. That is, they resist being 'persuaded' by another party to change their stance towards taking their own life. One way that practitioners are effective in these encounters, then, is by laying the interactional foundations for persons in crisis to make their own, agentive, independent decisions.

For instance, in Example 1.2, a negotiator ('N') proposes to a person in crisis ('PiC') that they are "completely in control".

```
Example 1.2: Crisis negotiation (simplified
transcript)
01   N:    But you can stop this. Can't you.
02   PiC:  No.
03   N:    You're- you can stop this.
04         (pause)
05   N:    You are completely in control.
06         (pause)
07   N:    You can stop this. You can
08         come down.
09         (pause)
10   PiC:  No.
11         (pause)
12   PiC:  I'm not coming down.
```

Despite the negotiator foregrounding the agency of the person in crisis, who "can stop this" (lines 03 and 07–08), the person in crisis rejects the negotiator's proposal directly (lines 10 and 12). It is quite amazing to know that this crisis will end with a positive outcome. The negotiator cannot and does not just give up. He will keep taking turns, knowing nothing about the mental life, suicidal ideation, personality, or many other 'factors' about the person in crisis. He does not have access to and so cannot use a psychological instrument to make such assessments. Even if he did, he cannot halt an encounter to initiate psychometric testing. The only evidence he has to develop a strategy is to use what the person in crisis does; what he says and how he says it.

In this way, every crisis encounter provides the basis for *a natural laboratory experiment* (Stokoe, 2018). Something *happens* after every turn that the person in crisis or the negotiator takes – one way or another. Someone may say one thing and it can be misunderstood, produce disagreement, conflict, or get no response. They may say another, and it makes sense or gets a productive answer.

Example 1.3 comes from a call to 911 emergency services in the USA. We join the call right from the start. We refer to the caller as 'CLR' and the dispatcher as 'DIS'. The dispatcher starts by identifying herself as 'Police' and then asking the caller "where" their emergency is.

```
Example 1.3: 911 call (simplified transcript)
01   DIS:  Police. This call is recorded.
02         Where is your emergency.
03   CLR:  Yeah ehm. It's on the top level
04         of the parking garage. An um it's
05         at the long distance uhm the
06         economy parking at Curtiss the
07         Flyers airport.
08   DIS:  What?
09   CLR:  The economy parking in the
10         Curtiss Flyers airport.
11   DIS:  Okay. What's the matter?
12            (pause)
13   CLR:  I need you to um… There's a
14         dead body.
15   DIS:  There's a dead body?
16   CLR:  In a car.
17   DIS:  In a car?
18   CLR:  Had been killed.
19   DIS:  What?
20            (pause)
21   DIS:  Hello?
```

While the caller has no problem in talking and gives precise information in response to the dispatcher's first question, it becomes clear as the conversation progresses that something is producing multiple misunderstandings. The dispatcher repeats, with a question in her voice, several of the answers given by the caller (lines 15, 17) as well as other turns that conversation analysts call 'open class repair initiators' ("What?" at lines 08 and 19, e.g., Drew, 1997), which indicate that something, without specifying what, was problematic in what came before. At line 20, it appears to the dispatcher that the caller has stopped participating in the interaction, and they attempt to restart it with another greeting, with an 'are you still there' querying intonation, at line 21 ("Hello?"). As the call unfolds, we discover, as does the dispatcher, that the caller is, in fact, calling to report their own 'dead body', as they intend to take their own life in the car park mentioned at the start of the call.

How do professionals deal with challenges like we have seen so far, from strong explicit resistance to unresponsiveness and disengagement, and from basic understanding to managing to keep taking turns in moments that are, quite bluntly, horrific? How do negotiators turn challenges into opportunities, to engage the person in crisis and potentially influence the choices they make? What are the tacit resources both negotiators and people in crisis have for justifying their presence and purpose, which tend to be diametrically opposed to each other? The stark contrasts between what the person in crisis wants and what the negotiators and dispatchers offer provide challenges, and negative consequences such as the person refusing to interact. This will be a recurrent theme throughout the book.

HOW DO WE KNOW WHAT WORKS?

Based on the brief examples we have presented thus far, what should the training manuals recommend in terms of next moves by practitioners in the face of resistance from people in crisis? As we will see in the next part of the chapter, while there is a great deal of research dedicated to understanding and improving crisis communication practice, there is little empirical, bottom-up scrutiny of real crisis encounters. Consequently, some of the training is wrong, or under-specified, to be helpful. We target this understanding by asking our core question, 'How do we know what works?'

This is a question we have posed throughout our research in recent years (e.g., Stokoe & Sikveland, 2017; Stokoe, 2011; 2013; 2014; 2018) that we have translated into training across many different workplace sectors. We have argued that communication skills training ought to be based on bottom-up studies of actual encounters, with recordings and analysis of conversations as they unfold. In the natural laboratory of real encounters, we are able to see the sometimes-multiple attempts made by police negotiators or dispatchers to move the conversation forwards. By comparing the precise design and sequential placement of failed and successful turns, we are able to specify what works.

Examples 1.4 and 1.5 illustrate what we mean by the 'natural laboratory. They show the failed (1.4) and then successful (1.5) start of a call between a person in crisis threatening suicide and a police negotiator. The person in crisis has, earlier that day, had an argument with another police officer (PC North not currently present) about an issue with the power supply to his house.

```
Example 1.4: Crisis negotiation (simplified
transcript)
01   PiC:  Hello?
02   N:    hello Kevin it's Steve. Thanks for
03         uh putting your phone back on,
04         uh I'd like to talk to you a bit
05         more about this PC North. Cos it's
06         obviously- it's- I mean it's something
07         that's very important to you.
08         It's important to me.
09         To find out what's going on.
10   PiC:  ((hangs up the phone))
```

```
Example 1.5: Crisis negotiation (simplified
transcript)
01   PiC: Yes hello.
02   N:    Hello Kevin it's Steve. Kevin can you
03         tell me a bit more about PC North
04         so I can do something about it.
```

```
05   PiC:   Right. Six months ago there was a- the
06          power company had a call
07          injunction to come in the
08          house ((continues))
```

The first attempt at opening is a failure. Our evidence is that the person in crisis says only an 'answering' hello before hanging up. He does not do a second 'greeting' hello and there are no 'how-are-yous'. Several components of N's turn do not work, including thanking PiC for putting his phone on, saying what he would like to do, saying what is important to PiC, and saying that PiC is important to N. There is also very little space for PiC to say anything.

However, N's second attempt at opening a conversation is successful. It looks very different. It erases much of the 'rapport-building' content we saw in the earlier attempt. He also asks what is often referred to (and therefore never recommended) in communication skills guidance as a 'closed-ended' (yes/no) question, replacing his more open-ended request to talk in the first attempt. Yet despite asking a yes/no question, PiC starts talking. N also focuses his question on action, and what can be done, rather than talking things through. By comparing N's failed and successful attempts to get PiC to talk, we can identify what works.

These examples illustrate what we will discover throughout the book: what works is not always what we think will work. A closed-ended question, without an attempt at rapport, is effective in this negotiation with a suicidal person in crisis. As conversation analysts, we collect instances of, say, negotiation openings, analysing each word-by-word, turn-by-turn. We then map different types of turns and patterns to different outcomes. Outcomes may be built into the very encounter being studied. They happen *inside* the encounter. A person says yes or no; talks or not; answers questions or does not; takes their own life or does not.

EXISTING LITERATURE ON CRISIS TALK

Over the past fifty years, crisis communication has been researched extensively, especially with hostage negotiation as a focus. Crisis negotiation has emerged as a large and interdisciplinary field, with a strongly applied focus from theory and experimentation to modelling and training. Psychologists, behavioural scientists, linguists and law enforcement professionals work together to understand and optimize crisis negotiation practice. Rubin (2016) outlines the history and evolution of crisis negotiation as research and practice, noting the broadening definition from hostage negotiation to crisis negotiation. Research questions are wide-ranging, from establishing the features of different types of hostage situations to the behavioural patterns and psychological attributes of negotiators (see Knowles, 2016 for an overview). In emergency calls, research examines cases of callers' resistance to questions (Whalen et al., 1988), navigating through emotional displays (Kidwell, 2006; Paoletti, 2012; Tracy & Tracy, 1998), and ways of recognizing when suicidal callers need peer support (Kevoe-Feldman & Iverson, 2022; for review of emergency call centre research see Kevoe-Feldman, 2019).

COMMUNICATION STRATEGIES FOR NEGOTIATING TOWARDS BEHAVIOUR CHANGE

There is a great deal of research dedicated to understanding and improving hostage and crisis negotiation practice. Much of this work is located in, or strongly influenced by, the psychology of social cognition and behavioural change. One of the most cited models for negotiation practice is the 'Behavioural Change Stairway Model' (BCSM). This model was developed by the FBI's Crisis Negotiation Unit, and outlines the relationship-building process involving the negotiator and subject, aiming to achieve a peaceful settlement of the critical incident (Vecchi, Van Hasselt, & Romano, 2005).

BCSM consists of five stages: active listening, empathy, rapport, influence, and behavioural change. The importance of the three first stages is intuitively sensible and compelling, and it seems natural that positive influence and behavioural change are more likely if the negotiator is able to first build a positive and trustworthy relationship. The first three stages overlap with almost any articulation of what counts as 'communication skills' across professional settings (e.g., mediation, counselling, police interviewing, medical encounters) and the model is referred to in numerous other popular science communication and negotiation books (e.g., Voss & Raz, 2016). 'Active listening', for example, is described in terms of uses of 'mirroring', 'summarizing', 'paraphrasing', 'emotional labelling', 'effective pauses', 'minimal encouragers', and 'open-ended questions' (e.g., Royce, 2005; Vecchi et al., 2005). This book provides some insight into what such 'skills' look like in real talk.

So far, there is little empirical, bottom-up scrutiny of real crisis encounters, and of how specific actions (questions, proposals, requests, etc., and their linguistic forms) build influence and behavioural change as observable 'shifts' in crisis conversations. Rubin (2016) notes that recommendations in the BCSM, such as 'rapport building' and 'influence', are 'amorphous and nebulous': "it is less clear what the linguistic features are that trainers can point to in order to help negotiators achieve" (p. 9). A handful of studies examine live, real cases of crisis negotiation (e.g., Charlés, 2007; Garcia, 2017; Rubin, 2016), but these remain the minority of the overall literature on communication in this field.

The crisis negotiation literature argues how question formats are relevant for bringing about positive or negative shifts in behaviour. For example, while the basic function of a question is to gain some information from an interlocutor, thereby driving the interaction forwards, a question can also challenge or refute a counterpart's argument or position (Miles, 2013). Researchers on crisis negotiation have thereby urged caution regarding the use of certain types of questions. For instance, James (2008, p. 52) recommends that crisis negotiators should not ask 'Why?' questions. He writes that "It is my contention that 'why' questions are generally poor choices for obtaining more information. Even though they may provide the client with an opening to talk more, they also make the client defend his or her actions." We find similar arguments elsewhere. For example, based on Goffman's 'face' theory, Tracy (2002) argues that investigative questions such as "did you see the shooting or only hear it?" evoke a threat to face when posed to emergency callers. In turn, callers may display belligerence in their response.

On the other hand, crisis negotiators who adopt, or 'mirror', the negotiatee's own terms have been found to be more successful in getting to a positive negotiation outcome. For example, Taylor and Thomas (2008), operationalizing 'mirroring' as 'linguistic style matching', or word-to-word correspondence between negotiator and negotiatee consecutive turns, found that negotiations were more likely to have a successful outcome when showing "reciprocation of positive affect, a focus on the present rather than the past, and a focus on alternatives rather than on competition" (p. 263). Such findings add some weight to the generally accepted position that crisis negotiators should not criticize or judge the person in crisis (Charlés, 2007), or otherwise challenge them. In contrast, Rogan (2011) suggests that, as problem solving is central to crisis management, it may be appropriate to challenge a suicidal person to "effectuate the subject's surrender" (p. 36). However, these studies do not provide empirical evidence of the linguistic and sequential specifics of the risky, and perhaps less risky, questions, requests or other actions relevant to behavioural change, and turning points. As the chapters in this book will reveal, particular ways of asking questions, and posing challenges, lead to positive rather than negative shifts in a person in crisis's stance towards the negotiation, and they do so systematically.

WHAT IS CONVERSATION ANALYSIS?

Before we describe what conversation analysis (CA) is, it may be useful to think about what a *conversation* is. Conversations are encounters with a landscape, with a start and an end like a racetrack. We start at the beginning with our recipient or recipients and, along the way, complete various projects. Think about the encounters you have with friends, partners, the check-out person at the supermarket, your children's schoolteacher, the doctor, a first date. Each of these has a landscape with projects, or actions, that comprise the complete encounter. Some actions will be the same, like greetings, openings, and closings. Others will be particular to the setting, like diagnoses, flirts, storytelling, complaints, requests, or instructions. We may move smoothly along the racetrack from one project to the next, or bump along the sides of the racetrack, on the rumble strips. The crisis talk racetrack is hard to join and progress along without many restarts and crashes, but their organization overall is nevertheless systematic, enabling us to identify its core component practices.

Conversation *analysis* is an academic science, originating in sociology, but crossing into psychology and linguistics. It was invented by three academics in the 1960s: Harvey Sacks, Emanuel Schegloff, and Gail Jefferson, and some of its foundational research is as strongly cited as much of the more popular psychological and linguistic research on human communication. Core to conversation analysis is its insistence on collecting actual, live, unfolding, talk in the wild. This is in stark contrast to much of the psychological and behavioural sciences which, despite being the main source of understanding of human behaviour, is surprisingly lite in studying people in the ordinary – and extraordinary – settings of their lives.

There are at least three related reasons why psychology and behavioural science – even social psychology and communication studies in general – have neglected to study people talking. The first is that, while most people inside and outside academic generally agree that communication, language, language behaviour, and so on, is important, psychologists and social scientists typically think of language as a tool to access the more important matters that lie behind our words – our attitudes, emotions, lies, prejudices, memories, and so on. Studying how people talk, and what they are doing when they talk, is apparently less informative. Yet we need only think of a phrase like, "I don't know" for the 'window-on-the-mind' metaphor to begin to unravel. Rather than assume that a person saying "I don't know" does not know (thus providing direct access to the brain) or does know (but is lying, and if only we find the right kind of tool we can still access the 'truth' lurking under the skull), conversation analysts examine how and when in talk such a phrase might crop up. And, much like other sorts of claims, like "I don't remember", they find that it often has nothing to do with knowing, or not knowing, but is doing something else entirely.

The second reason is that actual talk, and, thus, actual crisis talk, is often regarded as simply too messy to study. It is messy because we all talk differently: we have different accents, different turns of phrase, different idiomatic expressions, and our own verbal tics. At the same time, those who argue about the idiosyncratic nature of talk often also make sweeping generalizations about, say, how women or men talk – immediately homogenizing half of the world's population. The idea that real talk is too messy and disorganized to study – full of ums, uhs, pauses, false starts, and so on – has some academic credibility. The linguist Noam Chomsky argued that if we want to understand people's use of language, we must investigate their competence, not their performance. That is, we should investigate idealized language-in-theory, rather than messy language-in-use. Other linguists argued that this is a false dichotomy, not least because it excludes from inquiry data that is 'inconvenient to handle'.

The third reason why we know so little about real talk is a research myth we call the 'capturability' myth. By the capturability myth, we refer to the assumption that if we want to find out how people talk, the only way we can do this is by observing them, but that the fact of observation changes the naturally occurring behaviour we seek to examine. This is called the 'Observer's Paradox', or the 'Hawthorne effect'. The Observer's Paradox explains why recording live, unfolding conversation is an anathema to many scientists – what would the point be, when people just act for the camera? Instead, psychologists – and social scientists more broadly – rely on their tried and tested methods of laboratory experiments, simulation and *post-hoc* reports. But this assumes that how people talk behind a one-way mirror, under instruction to re-enact a 'conversation with friends', or 'conflict with a partner' is the same as real conversations with friends and partners. Conversation analysis shows that it is not. While extraneous variables can be controlled by the observer or experimenter in simulations, people's stake and interest in such encounters is not the same as when they are really having an argument. The only thing we learn when people report on their conversations on a survey or scale, or in an interview or focus group, is ... how people report on talk in research situations.

Much of psychology falls foul of what David Freedman calls 'the streetlight effect', or what others call 'the drunkard's search' – folklore for scientists. The story goes something like this: Late one evening, a police officer comes across a drunk man crawling around on the pavement, underneath a streetlight. The police officer asks him what he is doing. "Looking for my keys," replies the drunk. "Are you sure you dropped them here?" asks the officer. "No," replies the drunk – "I think it was more likely over there," and he points to a dark patch of pavement that is not lit up by the light. "Why are you looking here, then?" asks the officer. "Because this is where the light is", explains the man. Conversation analysts study the area of the street where the keys are; where the action is. Rather than ask people about their lives, or simulate them, or run experiments about them, we examine the lives we are interested in, as they are lived. How do words shape who we are? How can we avoid getting trapped in difficult conversations? In this book, a key question is how we can most effectively persuade or resist other people's actions.

There are many introductions to conversation analysis and we refer readers to those books for more depth (e.g., Clift, 2016; Schegloff, 2007; Sidnell, 2010; see also Stokoe, 2018, for a popular science introduction). While our book reports findings from CA research, we have attempted to reduce the amount of technical terminology to maximize accessibility. However, we outline some basic concepts. First, a fundamental observation of Sacks and his colleagues (Sacks, Schegloff, & Jefferson, 1974) is that conversations are made up of 'turns', and that these are arranged one after another. Of course, we have already seen that, while turns happen one after another, and that conversation comprises action-outcome pairs, it is not 'behaviourist' in orientation. At any point, a person in crisis (or anyone in any conversation) may, simply, do something other than what might be expected. However, we know what counts as 'expected' from the endogenous orientations of the participants. We could see that, in Extract 1.1, the negotiator expected the person in crisis to respond to a summons ("Mosi"), because the negotiator pursues a response, making its absence accountable.

Another core CA concept is 'turn design', which is to do with what goes *into* a turn. This depends on what action the turn is doing, and what is needed in terms of the "details of the verbal constructions through which that action is to be accomplished" (Drew, 2005, p. 83). A key premise is that conversation is not 'just talk'; it achieves the *actions* like inviting, accusing, joking, or offering "through which social life is conducted" (ibid., p. 75). Speakers 'analyse' the prior speaker's turn, the result of which "can be found in the construction of their fitted, responsive turn" (ibid): what CA calls the 'next turn proof procedure'. CA therefore examines how speakers orient to whatever has gone before and to what might come after (Heritage, 2005).

The final core CA concept we discuss here is 'sequence organization'. Conversational turns do not exist in isolation; they relate to each other "in systematically organized patterns of sequences of turns" (Drew, 2005, p.89). The basic building block to sequence organization is the 'adjacency pair'. When one speaker takes a turn, they do a first action, such that the recipient is expected to respond with a turn that delivers a second action paired with first one. Examples of adjacency pairs are 'question/answer', or 'offer/acceptance'. The production of the first part of an adjacency pair produces a context for the second part by making it conditionally relevant. That is to say, anything produced next is, for participants themselves, inspectable and accountable as an instance of that second pair part. So, on issuing an invitation, any response to it will be hearable as relevant to it, as being some kind of acceptance, rejection, stalling manoeuvre, account for non-acceptance, or whatever.

CA builds on participants' demonstrable understandings within the interaction itself, rather than from analysts' *a priori* definitions and assumptions of what to look for, or what 'should' happen. In CA, definitions of a relevant phenomenon to study emerge as a result of the early stages of the analysis. Starting with a technical transcript of the recorded data, CA proceeds by repeatedly viewing or listening to the data and transcript, and demonstrates, by analysing the organization of conversation turn by turn, how the design of an activity (e.g., requests, complaints, instruction) places constraints on the ways that responses can be made (e.g., Atkinson & Heritage, 1984). Each of the chapters in the book is built from an analysis of a collections of conversational phenomena. For example, in Chapter 5, we focus on what works to overcome resistance to the negotiation, including how negotiators and dispatchers may challenge persons in crisis in productive ways. To conduct the analysis, we identified sequences in the data in which we had observed a shift – positive or negative – in the stance taken by person in crisis towards the negotiation and towards staying alive rather than completing suicide. We tracked and compared the sequence and design features relevant to these shifts, focussing on how the shifts related to the professional party's previous and concurrent actions. We came to define a 'negative shift' as an intensified or maintained stance in the person in crisis's response; in contrast, a positive shift was a demonstrably weaker stance taken by the person in crisis to resist the negotiator.

This book will show that crisis talk is messy yet organized, full of idiosyncrasies yet systematic. It will show how people in crisis talk, rather than how we think they talk. It will show the payoffs to taking the time to capture and scrutinize real talk for understanding the power that language has, to push and pull the participants around; to constrain and compel them. We will show that while we hang onto myths like 'what happens in a negotiation mostly depends on the prior intentions of the person in crisis', we fail to examine what is actually happening during those negotiations.

HOW WE COLLECTED THE DATA AND USE IT ETHICALLY

Two datasets provide the empirical materials for our research. First, a UK police Hostage and Crisis Negotiation Unit supplied audio recordings of interactions between people in crisis and negotiators, recorded at the scene as a routine part of their job. The data were provided as part of a three-year study of crisis negotiation conducted between 2016 and 2018. The study is based on 14 individual cases (31 hours in total). In 13 cases, the person in crisis survived (including one where they were shot by the police), and in one case the person in crisis died from an accident at the end of the recording. Crisis negotiations are usually led by one negotiator, the primary or 'number one', who is supported by a team of other negotiators. The encounter is sometimes on the telephone and sometimes face-to-face, though also often at a distance – for instance, the person in crisis may be on a roof while the police negotiators are on the ground.

The second dataset comes from a USA 911 emergency call centre. Citizens phone to request emergency services for incidents ranging from car accidents to domestic disputes and suicide. The data were collected as part of a larger project of how 911 callers manage to give callers medical instruction in a time of crisis. From the larger collection, 35 calls were identified as suicide calls, of which 25 involved people calling because they feared a loved one was threatening suicide. Eight were from people who themselves report suicidal ideation or intent. Crucially, for the purposes of this book, both police negotiators and emergency dispatchers are in a similar position, talking to a person in crisis to influence their course of action. These two types of settings have not previously been compared, and we offer, for the first time, research exploring what communicative practices are effective, and ineffective, in both settings.

Working with actual recordings of the most important moment of a person's life – the moment where they may choose to stay alive or not – requires a high level of both formal ethical approval but also a high standard of ethical research practice. Lakeman and Fitzgerald (2009) note that "ethical problems and difficulties in obtaining approval to involve people who are suicidal in research has contributed to the current paucity of research that explores the suicidal experience" (p. 10); the research reported in this book is the first to explore live interactions with suicidal people in crisis.

In the case of the crisis negotiation dataset, data were supplied by the police hostage and crisis unit themselves, according to their own internal data management process and under a data sharing agreement. Like police interviews of suspects and witnesses, the recordings already existed, as they were made by police *in situ* as a standard (and, in the case of interviews, legally proscribed) part of working life. The recordings were provided to us after the possibility of formal consent (*pre-* or *post-hoc*) could be granted, and on the basis that they were used anonymously and stored according to the standards for university research data management (i.e., under encryption). Ethical approval was therefore secured on behalf of the Hostage and Crisis Negotiation Unit who supplied that data, and from Loughborough University Ethics Committee. In the case of the

911 recordings, the project received Institutional Review Board 'human subject approval' from Northeastern University's Ethics Committee, which included an approval letter to use the data for training and research from the participating Police.

Before we move on to describe the transcription system, it is worth considering the size of our datasets. We have 14 negotiations and 40 telephone calls. Do we have 'enough' data to warrant our claims? We argue that the answer is yes, for several reasons. First, conversation analysis is neither a quantitative nor qualitative method. It is sometimes both. The idea of 'one' negotiation, or 'one' telephone call, is not a useful way to think of the units of analysis in CA. One conversation contains many hundreds, or thousands, of questions, answers, overlaps, pauses, 'ums' and 'uhs'. An apparently 'single' instance delivers lots of instances of phenomena. In Schegloff's (1993, p. 101) words, "one is also a number, the single case is also a quantity, and statistical significance is but one form of significance". While claims based on large datasets are appealing, if there is a basic error in identifying the important phenomenon in the first place, Schegloff is correct to point out that "quantification is no substitute for analysis".

Second, conversation analysis is a form of logical analysis. An example from linguistics makes the point: the sentence "Peter forwarded the letter to his aunt Mary" is grammatical, and its grammar can be sensibly analysed. On the other hand, "To aunt the forwarded Peter letter Mary his" contains the same words but is not grammatical and has no structure. It is not a matter of counting how many times people say these things or asking how many people agree about their grammaticality. It is a matter of knowing how to speak English. We can make definitive analyses of these things based on just one example.

What makes a turn in conversation *analysable* is that it is recognizable and understandable by people, including analysts, who are members of a culture and a linguistic community that talk in those ways. We do not need huge samples and probabilistic statistics to do an analysis, even though we do need collections of instances of a phenomenon to analyse it, to figure out how it works. But even then, the analysis of each and every instance is done on the same basis, including recognizing something as an instance, which is the tacit ability that people have, and that anthropologists need, to understand the uses of their own natural language, or one in which they have acquired some competence.

Third, when people ask the 'how many' question, one way to respond is with an illustration to challenge the presuppositions built into it (Stokoe, 2018). For instance, how many black holes (or big bangs) does a physicist need to say something meaningful about the science of black holes? Most people laugh, and then say "one". So, how many negotiations with persons in crisis do we need to study before saying something meaningful about effective practice? How many times would we need to see that asking people to "talk" does not get people to talk? Our analysis is based on more than one case, but the logic and explanation remain the same.

Finally, quite simply, it would be strange to discount an analysis of a conversation because there is only one instance. Sometimes there may only be one instance to study. If you are at a party, and a guest collapses, hopefully you or someone else will call for an ambulance. If the ambulance takes a long time to arrive, and the guest dies, the telephone call will be a source of evidence in any subsequent investigation. In fact, this very situation was the subject of a classic conversation analytic study, showing the consequences 'When Words Fail' (Whalen & Zimmerman, 1999). Compared to the numbers of patients calling their GP receptionist, there are very few negotiations with suicidal persons in crisis, but it is important to know how they work.

WHY WE NEED TECHNICAL TRANSCRIPTS AND HOW TO READ THEM

All the recorded data analysed in this book are transcribed using a technical system developed by Jefferson (2004) and used universally for conversation analysis. The system is the first stage of analysis and cannot be reproduced by a machine. Like musical symbols, which notate pitch, pace, duration, and articulation of a note or passage of music, the system for transcribing conversation represents the pace, placement, intonational and prosodic features of words and phrases, turn by turn. Also like musical symbols, there is skill involved in 'hearing' a stretch of conversation (like a stretch of music) and rendering it accurately, such that another person can understand how the words were uttered, even if they do not have the recording itself.

Technical transcripts show us every detail of real talk: every pause, um, and uh. One reason for using this system is to enable the accurate representation of what people actually said, and how and when they said it, rather than 'tidy it up' or summarize it. In this way, it is a system that *ethically* reports the lived detail of people's encounters. Sometimes people complain that conversation analytic transcripts contain 'too much detail'. Continuing the music analogy, readers might be familiar with the quote, "too many notes, dear Mozart, too many notes", which is what Emperor Joseph II reportedly said after the first performance of Mozart's opera *Die Entführung aus dem Serail*, to which Mozart apparently replied, "Just as many as necessary, Your Majesty." Most verbatim transcripts render the detail of talk, sometimes including the actual words said, vulnerable to loss, omission, and alteration. Conversation analysts use a system that permits a forensic analysis of what actually happened, rather than editing how people talk and using impoverished versions for analysis, evidence, and commentary. This is especially important, one might argue, in legal settings. As Haworth (2018, p. 429) shows, writing about the routine contamination of recorded police evidence:

> the data are (unintentionally) distorted and misinterpreted as they pass through the criminal justice system. In stark contrast to the strict principles of preservation applied to physical evidence, … interview data go through significant alteration and contamination along the route from interview room to courtroom. They undergo various transformations in format, being converted between spoken and written modes and subject to various other processes along the way. Troublingly, the legal system treats all the different versions as unproblematic 'copies' of the original. This article will critically examine this process, highlighting the serious implications in terms of interference with criminal evidence;

something which is currently entirely unrecognised in the criminal justice system.

In order to explain the Jefferson system, we present a 'full' transcript, now, of a crisis negotiation example. Note that each example in this chapter has been numbered, 1.1, 1.2, 1.3, and so on. Each chapter's extracts will be numbered in this way, but the first number will be the chapter number (e.g., 2.1, 2.2; 3.1, 3.2, 3.3, and so on). Each example is also given a title. Each transcript has line numbers, a speaker identification letter, and then the transcript. All names are pseudonyms and we refer consistently throughout the book to 'N' for negotiator, 'N1', 'N2', etc. to differentiate primary and secondary (etc.) negotiators, 'DIS' for dispatcher, 'CT' for call taker, 'PiC' for person in crisis, and 'CLR' for 911 callers.

```
Example 1.6: I'm staying here
01   N:    Dalian. I'm he- (0.8) I am here
02         to help you.
03              (1.0)
04   N:    Okay,
05              (0.3)
06   N:    I wanna make sure that you- y- that
07         you're (0.2) you're okay, I want to
08         make sure that (.) that your (0.4)
09         your health is taken care of,
10              (1.0)
11   PiC:  I'm staying here.
12              (0.7)
13   N:    That's fine [you can stay there.]
14   PiC:              [I've given you my- ]
15         ONE HUNDRED percent- (.) when it-
16         becomes BLACK in the NIGHT, (0.2)
17         I'll be here.
```

In the transcript above, the symbols refer to the following features, as per the Jefferson (2004) system (see also Hepburn & Bolden, 2017):

Aspects of the relative placement/timing of utterances

=	Equals sign	Immediate latching of successive talk.
(0.8)	Time in parentheses	The length of a pause or gap, in tenths of a second.
(.)	Period in parentheses	A pause or gap that is discernible but less than a tenth of a second.
[overlap]	Square brackets	Mark the onset and end of overlapping talk.

Aspects of speech delivery

.	Period	Closing, usually falling intonation.
,	Comma	Continuing, slightly upward intonation.
?	Question mark	Rising intonation.
¿	Inverted question mark	Rising intonation smaller than that indicated by a question mark.
<u>Under</u>line	Underlining	Talk that is emphasized by the speaker.
Rea::lly	Colon(s)	Elongation or stretch of the prior sound. The more colons, the longer the stretch.
<u>o</u>:	Underlining preceding colon	When letters preceding colons are underlined the pitch rises on the letter and the overall contour is 'up-to-down'
<u>:</u>	Underlined colon	Rising pitch on the colon in an overall 'down-to-up contour
!	Exclamation mark	Animated tone.

-	Hyphen/dash	A sharp cut-off of the just prior word or sound.
↑	Upward arrow	Precedes a marked rise in pitch.
↓	Downward arrow	Precedes a marked fall in pitch.
<	'Greater than' sign	Talk that is 'jump-started'.
>faster<	'Lesser than' & 'greater Than' signs	Enclose speeded up or compressed talk.
<slower>	'Greater than' & 'lesser Than' signs	Enclose slower or elongated talk
LOUD	Upper case	Talk that is noticeably louder than that surrounding it.
°quiet °	Degree signs	Enclose talk that is noticeably quieter than that surrounding it.
huh/hah/heh/hih/hoh		Various types of laughter token.
(h)	'h' in parentheses	Audible aspirations within speech (e.g., laughter particles).
.hhh	A dot before an h or series of h's	An inbreath. (number of h's indicates length)
hhh	An h or series of h's	An outbreath/breathiness (number of h's indicates length)
#	Hash	Creaky voice
$ or £	Dollar or pound sign	Smile voice
*	Asterisk	Squeaky vocal delivery
( )	Empty single parentheses	Inaudible segment of talk.
(talk)	Word(s) in single parentheses	Transcriber's possible hearing.
(it)/(at)	A slash separating word(s) in single parentheses	Two alternative transcriber hearings
((laughs))	Word(s) in double parentheses	Transcriber comments or description of a sound

SUMMARY: INTERACTIONAL CHALLENGES AND OPPORTUNITIES IN CRISIS ENCOUNTERS

The opening chapter has introduced the problems that the book addresses (we know little about actual crisis talk; existing models and guidance may not actually specify what works) and given examples of the problems that professional police negotiators and dispatchers address as part of their daily work. We have summarized the literature in which the book sits and introduced our method of analysis and its technicalities. By trying to engage people in crisis to change their stance towards taking their own life, and returning to some kind of communicative stability, police negotiators and dispatchers face a range of interactional challenges. These challenges include managing strong emotions, resistance, hostility, and unresponsiveness. Based on our research on real interventions with suicidal persons in crisis, this book offers chapter-by-chapter evidence-based recommendations for effective negotiation practice. In crisis talk, every turn matters. Every turn affords and constrains. Every time, to stay alive.

REFERENCES

Atkinson, J. M., & Heritage, J. (Eds.). (1984). *Structures of social action*. Cambridge: Cambridge University Press.

Charlés, L. L. (2007). Disarming people with words: Strategies of interactional communication that crisis (hostage) negotiators share with systemic clinicians. *Journal of Marital and Family Therapy, 33*, 51–68.

Clift, R. (2016). *Conversation analysis*. Cambridge: Cambridge University Press.

Drew, P. (1997). 'Open' class repair initiators in response to sequential sources of troubles in conversation. *Journal of Pragmatics, 28*(1), 69–101.

Drew, P. (2005). Conversation analysis. In Fitch, K. L. & Sanders, R. E. (Eds.), *Handbook of language and social interaction* (pp. 71–102). Psychology Press.

Garcia, A. (2017). What went right: Interactional strategies for managing crisis negotiations during an emergency service call. *The Sociological Quarterly, 58*, 495–518.

Haworth, K. (2018). Tapes, transcripts and trials: The routine contamination of police interview evidence. *The International Journal of Evidence & Proof, 22*(4), 428–450.

Hepburn, A., & Bolden, G. B. (2017). *Transcribing for social research*. London: Sage.

Heritage, J. (2005). Conversation analysis and institutional talk. In Fitch, K. L. & Sanders, R. E. (Eds.), *Handbook of language and social interaction* (pp. 103–148). Psychology Press.

Ireland, C. A., & Vecchi, G. M. (2009). The Behavioral Influence Stairway Model (BISM): A framework for managing terrorist crisis situations? *Behavioral Sciences of Terrorism and Political Aggression, 1*(3), 203–218.

James, R. K. (2008). *Crisis intervention strategies.* Belmont, CA: Thompson Brooks/Cole

Jefferson, G. (2004). Glossary of transcript symbols. *Conversation analysis: Studies from the first generation,* 24–31.

Kevoe-Feldman, H. (2019). Inside the emergency service call-center: Reviewing thirty years of language and social interaction research. *Research on Language and Social Interaction, 52*(3), 227–240.

Kevoe-Feldman, H., & Iversen, C. (2022). Approaching institutional boundaries: Comparative conversation analysis of practices for assisting suicidal callers in emergency and suicide helpline calls. *Journal of Pragmatics.*

Kidwell, M. (2006). 'Calm down!': The role of gaze in the interactional management of hysteria by the police. *Discourse Studies, 8*(6), 745–770.

Knowles, G. J. (2016). Social psychological dynamics of hostage negotiation: Forensic psychology, suicide intervention, police intelligence/counterintelligence, and tactical entry. *Journal of Criminal Psychology, 6,* 16–27.

Lakeman, R., & M. Fitzgerald. (2009). Ethical suicide research: A survey of researchers. *International Journal of Mental Health Nursing, 18,* 10–17.

Miles, E. W. (2013). Developing strategies for asking questions in negotiation. *Negotiation Journal, 29,* 383–412.

Nisbett, R. E., & Wilson, T. D. (1977). Telling more than we can know: Verbal reports on mental processes. *Psychological Review, 84*(3), 231.

Paoletti, I. (2012). The issue of conversationally constituted context and localization problems in emergency calls. *Text & Talk, 32*(2), 191–210.

Rogan, R. G. (2011). Linguistic style matching in crisis negotiations: A comparative analysis of suicidal and surrender outcomes. *Journal of Police Crisis Negotiations, 11,* 20–39.

Royce, T. (2005). The negotiator and the bomber: analyzing the critical role of active listening in crisis negotiations. *Negotiation Journal, 21,* 5–27.

Rubin, G. R. (2016). *Negotiation power through tag questions in crisis negotiations.* Unpublished Masters Thesis.

Sacks, H., Schegloff, E. A., & Jefferson, G. (1974). A simplest systematics for the organization of turn taking for conversation. In Schenkein, J. (Ed.), *Studies in the organization of conversational interaction* (pp. 7–55). Academic Press.

Schegloff, E. A. (1993). Reflections on quantification in the study of conversation. *Research on Language and Social Interaction, 26*(1), 99–128.

Schegloff, E. A. (2007). *Sequence organization in interaction.* Cambridge University Press.

Sidnell, J. (2010). The ordinary ethics of everyday talk. *Ordinary ethics: Anthropology, language, and action,* 123–139.

Stokoe, E. (2011). Simulated interaction and communication skills training: The 'conversation-analytic role-play method'. In Antaki, C. (Ed.), *Applied conversation analysis* (pp. 119–139). Basingstoke: Palgrave Macmillan.

Stokoe, E. (2013). The (in) authenticity of simulated talk: Comparing role-played and actual interaction and the implications for communication training. *Research on Language & Social Interaction, 46*(2), 165–185.

Stokoe, E. (2014). The Conversation Analytic Role-play Method (CARM): A method for training communication skills as an alternative to simulated role-play. *Research on Language and Social Interaction, 47*(3), 255–265.

Stokoe, E. (2018). *Talk: The science of conversation.* London: Hachette UK.

Stokoe, E., & Sikveland, R. O. (2017). The conversation analytic role-play method. In Pink, S. Fors, V. & O'Dell, T. (Eds.), *Theoretical scholarship and applied practice* (pp. 73–96). New York: Berghahn Books.

Stokoe, E., Humă, B., Sikveland, R. O., & Kevoe-Feldman, H. (2020). When delayed responses are productive: Being persuaded following resistance in conversation. *Journal of Pragmatics, 155,* 70–82.

Taylor, P. J., & S. Thomas. (2008). Linguistic style matching and negotiation outcome. *Negotiation and Conflict Management Research, 1,* 263–281.

Tracy, S. J. (2002). When questioning turns to face threat: An interactional sensitivity in 911 call-taking. *Western Journal of Communication, 66,* 129–157.

Tracy, K., & Tracy, S. J. (1998). Rudeness at 911: Reconceptualizing face and face attack. *Human Communication Research, 25*(2), 225–251.

Vecchi, G. M., Van Hasselt, V. B., & Romano, S. J. (2005). Crisis (hostage) negotiation: Current strategies and issues in high risk conflict resolution. *Aggression and Violent Behavior, 10,* 533–551.

Voss, C., & Raz, T. (2016). *Never split the difference: Negotiating as if your life depended on it.* Random House.

Whalen, J., Zimmerman, D. H., & Whalen, M. R. (1988). When words fail. A single case analysis. *Social Problems, 35*(4), 335–362.

Crisis talk, from practice to training

Getting the conversation started

Chapter 2

WHAT IS THIS CHAPTER ABOUT?

Having sketched out the core interactional challenges of crisis management in Chapter 1, we now explore how professionals start dealing with these challenges in the opening phases of an encounter. We will consider how opening a crisis negotiation departs radically from the opening of almost any other encounter. While the start of any conversation can immediately involve conflict ("Where have you been all morning?"), confusion ("Is that the vets?"; "Hello? Can you hear me?"), or a level of urgency or crisis ("did you leave the oven on?"), a distinctive feature of crisis negotiations is that the person in crisis might simply say nothing at all. This creates a very basic challenge for negotiators, who must keep taking opening turns ("Hello", "My name's James", "I'm one of

DOI: 10.4324/9780429354892-2

the negotiators", "I'm here to help", "Hello?") until, eventually, the person in crisis joins the conversation. In this chapter we identify ways of engaging persons in crisis.

We ask:

What strategies can negotiators use to increase the likelihood of a person in crisis joining the conversation beyond the opening turns of talk?

WHY IS THIS TOPIC IMPORTANT?

When dealing with people in crisis who appear unwilling to engage in a conversation, crisis negotiators must create opportunities to engage rather than disengage. Every turn of talk is an opportunity for engagement, starting from the first turns in a conversation. For example, a first hook, or topic, could emerge in a conversation's opening stages, enticing someone to continue. But securing the first topic can also fail, in which case the person in crisis hangs up the telephone or disengages in other ways, and the conversation terminates prematurely. Negotiators need to minimize the risk of such early, premature ends to the conversation, and in this chapter, we demonstrate how they do so.

WHAT CURRENT TRAINING TELLS US ABOUT OPENING A NEGOTIATION

As others have observed, opening a crisis negotiation "involves a great deal *more than* merely picking up a telephone and initiating a conversation" (McMains & Mullins, 2014, p. 243, emphasis added). And opening a face-to-face encounter certainly involves more than appearing physically in front of the person in crisis. But what exactly constitutes these 'more than' features that get conversations started on the right footing? Strentz (2018) acknowledges that openings of crisis encounters may be filled with "confusion and miscommunication" (p. 52). Yet we understand very little about or the detail of how confusion and miscommunication come about in real encounters as they unfold.

Current recommendations for starting a crisis encounter, and establishing rapport and trust with the person in crisis, include *self-introductions* such as, "my name is…" and "I am with the…

department", and *status checks*, "Is everything under control over there? Has anyone been hurt?" (Strentz, 2018). Strentz (2018) also highlights the relevance of being:

(i) Personal (by providing your name)
(ii) Professional and authoritative (by providing affiliation)
(iii) Concerned with the welfare of everyone involved.

While the latter advice is relevant to hostage situations, such beginnings also extend to crisis encounters with individuals. Miller (2005) argues for a simple introduction and statement of purpose at the beginning of negotiations to instil confidence and credibility. Beyond the first introductions, negotiation training next emphasizes the importance of establishing a conversation from the person in crisis's point of view. If a negotiator engages with a person in crisis and they begin "a conversation talking about his dog or parakeet, this is where we should begin" (Roberts, 2005, p. 158). Such methods reinforce a key strategy for engaging with a person in crisis to talk on their terms first, and keep the conversation moving forward. However, when someone is reluctant to start a conversation, the way to launch such first topics might take a long time.

To get a sense of how negotiators can overcome or prevent barriers to communication, such as the person in crisis hanging up, disengaging, or escalating the crisis, we begin with a contrastive look at the routine flow of ordinary telephone openings. Everyday conversations teach us that there is an orderly organization to talk. People can find many opportunities at the start of a conversation for doing things like asking for help, making an announcement, or calling with bad news. By understanding that talk is orderly, we can identify the key opportunities to help negotiators overcome and manage the challenge of starting a conversation with someone who does not want to engage. By understanding the general landscape of social interaction, we can build a stronger empirical position from which to understand the barriers to establishing and maintaining a conversation, and how to avoid them.

HOW OPENINGS OF CRISIS NEGOTIATIONS DIFFER FROM OTHER TYPES OF CONVERSATIONS

Introductions are a key element for opening a crisis encounter. This considers what features characterize conversational openings in this environment and what makes opening a crisis encounter more challenging than opening other encounters. We begin by showing how crisis openings share the same organization as openings in more mundane settings. By establishing the foundation for starting a conversation, we can identify recurrent, systematic patterns of a routine method, giving a baseline for identifying interactional challenges particular to crisis negotiation.

To understand how openings are structured, we present a case from an ordinary domestic call between two American friends, Hyla and Nancy (Example 2.1). The call comes from a collection made before caller ID. Therefore, callers rely on other forms of identification, such as saying their names or voice recognition (Schegloff, 1968). In this example, Hyla is calling Nancy; her dialling (line 01) serves as the summons that initiates the conversation. Nancy responds to the summons by picking up the phone and saying, "Hello:?" (line 02), and this is the first sequence of the conversational opening.

```
Example 2.1: Hyla and Nancy
01                    ((ring))
02    Nancy:          Hello:?
03    Hyla:           Hi:,
04    Nancy:          HI::.
05    Hyla:           How are you hh.=
06    Nancy:          =Fi:ne how're you.
```

Hyla and Nancy's conversation unfolds following Nancy's "Hello:?". When Hyla says, "Hi:," (line 03), she delivers a *greeting* while simultaneously *recognizing* her friend's voice. At line 04, Nancy gives a second greeting, but it sounds very different from her answering-the-phone, "Hello:?". This time, the "HI::." is louder, brighter, and more animated. It conveys recognition of Hyla's voice in return. Next, Hyla and Nancy exchange 'how-are-yous'

Table 2.1 Canonical sequence of opening actions.

---

1. **The summons and answer** (Example 2.1, lines 01–02)
2. **The greetings and identification** (Example 2.1: for Hyla and Nancy, just the sound of the voice is enough for identification at lines 03–04)
3. **The initial enquiries** (Example 2.1: the 'how-are-yous' at lines 05–06).

(lines 05–06). Hyla and Nancy exchange 'how-are-yous' rapidly and reciprocally. The speed of exchange is represented by the equals signs ('='), which indicate that the two turns are 'latched' together.

Conversation analysts have shown that, across settings including phone calls, face-to-face encounters, Skype calls, and even instant messaging, conversations recurrently open with three rapid, reciprocal, component pairs of actions (Stokoe, 2018). Table 2.1 presents this systematic order of openings: this sequence of actions proves robust across opening sequences, whether on the telephone or face-to-face (Stokoe, 2018). We will keep this in mind as we explore openings of crisis encounters later on.

There are numerous instances where conversation openings look quite different from the sequence in Table 2.1 – at least on the surface. For example, in various institutional telephone calls, where the caller and the call-taker do not know each other, participants do more work to achieve mutual recognition. However, we can still identify a similar sequence of opening actions, as it were, 'behind the surface.' In Example 2.2, a patient is phoning their general practice to book an appointment to see a doctor.

```
Example 2.2: Patient and doctors' reception
01                    ((ring))
02    Recep:    >Good< mornin:g,
03              surgery: Cath speaking,
04                    (1.6)
05    Patient:  Hello have you got an
06              appointment for
07              Frida:y afternoon or
08              teatime please.
```

The parties greet each other (">Good< mornin:g,", line 02, and "Hello", line 05), but, in this opening moment, only the receptionist provides identification of both the department, surgery, and her first name, Cath. The patient's identity is relevant later; for now, the main action is making an appointment. Typical for organizational encounters, we find no rounds of 'how-are-yous,' as the patient proceeds from her greeting ("Hello") straight into the reason for her call.

In Example 2.3 the opening proceeds in a similar manner where a salesperson has phoned a local company. Again, the caller quickly moves from the greeting ("Hi", line 06) with the reason for their call.

```
Example 2.3: Salesperson calling a business
01                 ((ring))
02   Business:  Good afternoon,
03              =Advance Services
04              Management,
05                (.)
06   Sales:     Hi.=↑Can I: (0.5)
07              ↓speak with John
08              Stornoway please.
```

In Example 2.4 a caller greets the windows and doors representative before launching a quote request.

```
Example 2.4: Customer calling a business
01 Windows:   G'd afternoon, ↑Fine Bar ↑Wi:ndows,
02               (0.6)
03 Customer:  .shih (.).hh >hi< w'd it be
04            ↑po:ssible f'somebody t'come
05            an' give me a quote on uh: a
06            window an: some doors please.
```

In Example 2.5 we see how a sense of urgency might also define openings of phone calls to family members: in this case the Mum calls the daughter to check whether she got into the house without setting off the alarm. We see the urgency in that the Mum, following a greeting in line 04, jumps straight into the reason for her call in lines 06–07, in overlap with the Daughter's "Hi::" (line 05).

```
Example 2.5: Semi-urgent call from Mum to Daughter
01                      ((ring))
02    Daughter: hHello:?
03                      (0.4)
04    Mum:      .pt Hiya £sweetie,£=it's only me,
05    Daughter: h[Hi::]
06    Mum:        [.pt ] did'ya get in #u-an': unlock
07                the ala:rm?
```

The form call openings take varies, then, depending on contingencies like who is calling whom, whether or not speakers know each other, the urgency of the situation, and so on. As conversation analysts have repeatedly shown, these are not random, messy variations, but systematic ones, by which we construct and recognize the particular nature of each type of call (Stokoe, 2018). Therefore, the sequence of opening actions presented above is still relevant to all different types of encounters: it is based on these structures that we can quickly recognize what kind of encounter it is we are dealing with and adjust our behaviours accordingly. Whereas a greeting from a casual call between friends might have rounds of greetings and how are you's, organizational settings tend to be more formalized, with fewer rounds of greetings and a move straight to the call's business.

As we will see next, in Example 2.6, the openings of crisis negotiations are reduced, and reciprocal greetings of any type are routinely absent.

```
Example 2.6: Crisis negotiation opening #1
01                    ((ring))
02    PiC:    Ye=hello:.
03    N:      Hello Kevin=it's Steve.
04            (1.0)
05    N:      .hh Kevin- (.) can you tell me: a
06            bit more about pee cee North
07            so I can do something about it.
```

In Example 2.6, the one answering the phone is the person in crisis (PiC) and picks up the phone in response to the summons (telephone ringing, line 01). Here the summons response takes the form of a "Ye=hello:" (a fast succession of "yeah" followed by "hello"). Then, the caller (negotiator: N) responds with a greeting ("Hello") and the naming of PiC, followed by N's self-identification (line 03). In this case, N shows they know who they are talking to but does not assume that PiC will recognize them by voice, so he/she provides their name to secure mutual recognition of who is calling.

Usually, and as we saw in the previous examples, a greeting can be followed by a *reciprocal* greeting, especially if the parties know each other (Examples 2.1 and 2.5), or a reason for the call can immediately follow if they don't know each other (Examples 2.2–4). Here, neither of these events occurs. N's initial inquiry occurs only after a one-second gap (line 04), during which the caller (PiC) does not show acceptance to join the conversation and leaves a slot open for N to say more without inviting it in any encouraging way. This is typical of crisis encounters: a person in crisis does not reciprocate a greeting, or in other ways, facilitate a smooth path into a conversation.

The same pattern emerges in openings of face-to-face crisis interactions. In Example 2.7, the current, transitioning, primary negotiator (NX) hands the negotiation over to the new primary negotiator – N1. NX introduces N1 as he arrives at the scene. At this moment, the negotiator greets PiC by name (line 04). We see that PiC does not answer at line 05.

Example 2.7: Crisis negotiation opening #2
```
01   NX:      Hi Oliver,=There's somebody else
02            who wants to say hello to you,
03               (0.4)
04   N1:      Hi Oliver?
05               (0.8)
```

Following this gap, the negotiator proceeds by introducing himself by name (line 06):

Example 2.7: Crisis negotiation opening #2 (cont'd)
```
06   N1:      My name is Chris.
07               (1.0)
08   N1:      One of the negotiators?
09               (1.9)
```

Again, there is no answer from PiC (who is within hearing range) for an entire second, then N1 provides some information on his institutional role, continuing on the sentence he already started: "My name is Chris … (1.0)… One of the negotiators?" (lines 06–08). Here we see that in the absence of a response, negotiators keep pursuing one, and consequently, steps 1 to 3 in the sequence of opening actions (Table 2.1) do not unfold in a typical way.

So far, we have seen that while providing a greeting and self-introduction, negotiators do not get a reciprocal response from the person in crisis. The absent greeting from PiC is evident in the interaction, as different from 'normal' conversation, and is something that negotiators routinely experience. As negotiators train and learn how to open a negotiation 'on the job,' they understand differences between crisis encounters and other encounters. Since negotiators have a similar point of reference for what's 'normal' in everyday conversation, they use this tacit knowledge as a point of departure when learning how to communicate as negotiators. To understand what might constitute such an implicit learning process, we differentiate what is 'normal', or expected, in routine social interaction, from the knowledge and experience negotiators have as they encounter individual persons in crisis.

Our research shows the tacit experience that negotiators may already have in reaching out to someone who does not necessarily want to engage in dialogue. For example, in Examples 2.6 and 2.7, the negotiator appears unphased by the lack of a return greeting. Whether or not negotiators are accustomed to persons in crisis not returning a greeting, or in other ways reciprocate the opening actions put forward by the negotiators, negotiators routinely have to deal with some form of resistance early in the conversation. Later in this chapter, we explore how negotiators deal with this challenge interactionally. Next, we show how negotiators may best introduce themselves, by name or by affiliation to get the conversation started.

SHOULD NEGOTIATORS AVOID ASSOCIATING THEMSELVES WITH THE POLICE?

We have established that the first hurdle of crisis negotiation is opening the conversation. We now address how a person in crisis, though they resist the conversation in the first place, ends up engaging in a conversation.

One strategy commonly observed is the negotiator's self-introduction by name. Of course, what is absent in using the first name is the person's professional identity, for example, 'the police', a category some negotiators avoid mentioning in the opening of the negotiations. We find the omission of a professional identity unnecessary. Negotiators are better off making their affiliation with the police known, and not trying to hide their institutional identity. While negotiators may have many reasons to disassociate with the police, they are *with* the police, and this is not worth hiding from the person in crisis. Our research shows that being open about institutional affiliation, e.g., "I'm with the police", is effective for getting beyond introductions in the negotiation. We turn to Example 2.8 to demonstrate our point. N has just arrived at the scene where the person in crisis barricaded herself inside her flat.

```
Example 2.8: Who are you #1
01   N:        Hi darling.
02              (.)
03   N:        My n- my name is David.
04              (0.6)
05   N:        Uh[m    ]
06   PiC:         [Who ] are you,
07              (0.2)
08   N:        I'm just here to try and help.
09              (0.7)
```

Following an unanswered greeting (line 02), N introduces himself by name in line 03: "my name is David.". PiC responds, "Who are you," (line 06) in place of reciprocating a greeting or self-identification by name. At the same time, since N has already presented himself by name, PiC makes the negotiator accountable for not providing relevant information about their identity. In response, N formulates his purpose or role: "I'm just here to try and help." (line 08).

We find a similar exchange in Example 2.9:

```
Example 2.9: Who are you #2
01   N:        My- my name is Riley=I just want
02              to talk to you.
03              (0.9)
04   PiC:      Who are you.
05              (1.0)
06   N:        I'm with the polic:e.=But I
07              want to talk to you.=Try and
08              help you.
09              (2.0)
```

Again, N introduces himself by name: "My name is Riley" (line 01). And despite N's account for his presence, "I just want to talk to you" (lines 01–02), PiC makes N accountable for not having provided a satisfactory role or purpose, by asking, "Who are you." (line 04). In response, N specifies his professional role "I'm with the polic:e." (line 06), but immediately followed by a reformulation of his account in line 01: "But I want to talk to you.=Try and help you." (lines 06–08).

In Examples 2.8–9 we have seen that negotiators prioritize presenting themselves with name and a proposal to "talk" and "help", thereby potentially withholding their association with the police. To better understand this dynamic, we turn first to what happens next in the interaction, then consider negotiators' conceptualizations of 'police' versus the purpose of initiating dialogue with the person in crisis.

The next turns following Example 2.8 confirm our impression that the negotiators avoid self-categorizing as 'police' and whatever might be associated with such a category.

```
Example 2.8 (cont'd): Who are you #1
10   PiC:     Yeah. Who are you.=You know
11            from where.
12               (0.3)
13   N:       Oh- I- I'm from the police.
14               (.)
15   N:       But my job is to sit here and
16            talk to you and try and help.
17               (0.4)
18   N:       See what we can do to help ya.
19               (0.5)
20   PiC:     You ca:n't. I'm dying tonight
21            (real soon).
```

PiC unpacks her question "Who are you", by specifying, "You know from where" (lines 10–11). N provides his professional identity ('police', line 13), but promptly contrasts this identity with a formulation of purpose to talk and help: "But my job is to sit here and talk to you and try and help." (lines 15–16). The "but" here puts 'police' in direct contrast with N's version of why they are there. The "oh" in line 13 is particularly revealing of the delay with which the negotiator admits he is from the police: a small but powerful word we use to show that something someone was saying or asking did not occur to us until the moment right before the "oh" gets produced (see Heritage, 1984). Also revealing is the negotiators' use of "I [am] just" (line 08 in Example 2.8; line 01 in Example 2.9): "just" here functions to restrict and contrast the negotiators' role about something else, possibly what the person in crisis may think, or accuse, the negotiators of doing.

People, including negotiators and people in crisis, operate with pre-established notions of what a category of professionals represent. The negotiators are here observably attempting to deal with, or pre-empt, potential resistance towards the category 'police,' by highlighting the gentle and rapportful approaches of 'talk' and 'help' instead. One might expect 'police' to undermine the purpose of the negotiation. However, our research shows that this is not necessarily the case when opening a negotiation. We demonstrate that negotiators are better off providing their professional identity (i.e., "I'm with the police") initially, then moving on with the conversation. Examples 2.10 and 2.11 help illuminate this point further.

In Example 2.10, as N2 arrives at the scene and PiC asks, "Who's he" (line 03), N2 suggests N1 introduces him as "with the police" (line 05), which N1 then answers to PiC (line 08). In the next turn, lines 10–11, N1 requests that PiC move into visibility, which we can gather PiC does next. In other words, there is no evidence here that PiC is resisting further engagement in the negotiation because N2 is 'with the police'.

```
Example 2.10: I'm with the police #1
01    N1:      Hello Patrick?
02                  (0.5)
03    PiC:     Who's he
04                  (1.9)
05    N2:      °°I'm with the police, just
06             tell him°°
07                  (0.4)
```

```
08   N1:    He's with the police Patrick,
09               (0.5)
10   N1:    I like speaking to you,=it's a
11          lot better when you come round there,
12               (3.0)
13   N1:    Right, (0.5) Patrick? Just for
14          your information, my colleague
15          is going.=One of my colleagues
16          is going and (he) t- he's
17          got another one he:re. Who's
18          looking after: (0.4)
19   PiC:   °Right°.
```

Example 2.11 is another case of the negotiator volunteering their association with the police straight away. This example is from the opening of a telephone call. N first introduces herself by name (line 01), then proceeds with "I'm with the police" and the reason for her call (line 03). PiC accepts "Okay." (line 06) and turns out to be responsive to N1's "are you all right in there," with "Yeah I'm fine." (line 11).

```
Example 2.11: I'm with the police #2
01   N1:    Hiya. My- my name's Vicky:.
02               (0.7)
03   N1:    I- I'm with the police. They s-
04          they said I was gonna ca:ll?
05               (1.8)
06   PiC:   Okay.
07               (0.2)
08   N1:    C- (.) hi are you all right
09          in there,
10               (0.8)
11   PiC:   Yeah I'm fine.
```

The category 'police' also works better than 'negotiator', as evidenced by the following case in Example 2.12. Here we see that, when negotiators introduce themselves as "negotiator", a person in crisis may resist this category on the basis that "they are not robbing a bank". Implicitly, PiC here treats a negotiator as an inappropriate category of professionals dealing with individuals in crisis.

```
Example 2.12: I'm not robbing a bank
01   N1:     Hi Oliver,=There's somebody
02           else who wants to say hello to you,
03                (0.4)
04   N2:     Hi Oliver?
05                (0.8)
06   N2:     My name is Chris.
07                (1.0)
08   N2:     One of the negotiators?
09                (1.9)
10   N2:     Just seeing if we can.hhh help
11           you come down safely, (0.6)
12           and we can sort this out.
13                (0.3)
14   PiC:    (Then) why is there a negotiator.
15                (1.0)
16   PiC:    There's nothing to negotiate.
17                (2.2)
18   PiC:    I'm not robbing a bank, Why
19           is there a nego- negotiator here.
```

LESSONS ABOUT FIRST INTRODUCTIONS

- There is no evidence that "I'm with the police" is either rejected, escalated, or challenged, by the person in crisis.
- Actively withholding institutional affiliation is counter-productive to getting the conversation started. Negotiators

can identify themselves as "with the police" and be upfront about their affiliation.

We are now ready to move beyond the first introductions and see how negotiators effectively deal with early resistance towards proceeding with the conversation.

HOW TO GET PAST EARLY RESISTANCE

Having presented early challenges of getting the conversation started, in this section, we offer conversational strategies to get a person in crisis to engage with the negotiator productively, rather than reject the negotiator's attempt to proceed beyond the opening phase of the conversation. We show that asking questions is vital, specifically, questions (i) in the person in crisis's domain, and (ii) that do not challenge the person in crisis's choices.

Giving purpose to negotiation by proposing to 'help' and 'talk' is not as straightforwardly acceptable as it may sound. Example 2.13 suggests how formulations of 'help' and 'talk' are easily rejected by the person in crisis, based on their irrelevance. PiC has barricaded herself in her flat, threatening to asphyxiate using a noose around her neck.

```
Example 2.13: I'm dying tonight
01   PiC:    Yeah. Who are you.=You know
02           from where.
03               (0.3)
04   N:      Oh- I- I'm from the police.
05               (.)
06   N:      But my job is to sit here and
07           talk to you and try and help.
08               (0.4)
09   N:      See what we can do to help ya.
10               (0.5)
11   PiC:    You ca:n't. I'm dying tonight
12           (real soon).
```

We address the matter on how persons in crisis respond to proposals of 'help' and 'talk' in more detail in Chapter 3 and show how such proposals are not only likely to be rejected – persons in crisis actively draw on these word choices when displaying explicit rejection of the negotiation. For now, we note that persons in crisis tend to provide some reasoning for rejecting 'help' and proceed to show how negotiators may productively move on from there. First of all, negotiators manage resistance with questions.

THE POWER OF ASKING QUESTIONS

Generally, questions set clear constraints on what is relevant to happen next in the interaction (Clayman & Heritage, 2002). They may do so in a non-threatening way without the one asking the question having to push too hard. Consider example 2.14, including the turns following PiC's strong rejection, "You can't save me.".

```
Example 2.14: What's made it bad tonight
01  PiC:    You can't save me.
02              (0.9)
03  N:      What's made it- (.) what's made it
04          really bad tonight though Jessica.=
05          What's made
06          i[t- what's made it [so bad. ]
07  PiC:    [Just e-            [just eve]rythi:ng.
08  PiC:    Just everything.=(n) you know,
09          just- just- just -just- just it all.
10              (2.2)
```

In lines 03–04 N asks, "What's made it- (.) what's made it really bad tonight though Jessica.", which opens for anything which PiC might want to highlight as a reason for her choices, while not in any way threatening those choices. The reason PIC gives in lines 07–09 does not provide any specifics ("just everything"), yet as an answer to the question provides N with an opportunity to ask again. Following a gap of 2.2 seconds (line 10), the question is still 'hanging in the air' unanswered, as both N and PiC show in their respective next turns:

```
Example 2.14: What's made it bad tonight (cont'd)
11   PiC:   Ju[st- just- ] just- just it all.
12   N:        [Like what.]
13              (0.2)
14   N:     Like what.
15              (0.3)
16   PiC:   Just
17              (4.7)
18   PiC:   Just- just
19              (3.5)
```

We can see that PiC has started an answer and that N allows for the time it takes: N awaits a response after each turn (see the gaps at lines 22, 25, 27, and 30), then pursues his initial request for PiC to "tell him" what has happened. Eventually, in line 31, PiC starts talking about her grandmother ("nan") being the "last friend I ever h:ad alive".

```
Example 2.14: What's made it bad tonight (cont'd)
20   N:     So we- we know- (.) we know can
21          deal with the whole James thing.
22              (0.3)
23   N:     That's fine. That- that'll be
24          easy to deal with.
25              (0.3)
26   N:     Tell me about the other stuff then.
27              (1.1)
28   N:     Tell me about the other stuff
29          that's made you feel so bad tonight.
30              (1.6)
31   PiC:   My nan (.) ~(was really) the
32          last friend I ever h:ad alive~,
```

The conversation reaches a point where N and PIC are on board with the topic launched. And it is not just any topic: it is a topic within PiC's domain of expertise and knowledge. N is still in a position of not knowing about PIC. Still, N can use this 'unknowing' position productively to display an interest in learning more about PiC and her relationship with her grandmother. In this way, N can portray themselves as someone who does not have all the answers regarding PiC, but still wants to learn more. The first topic is now a hook that N can use to progress the conversation and support PiC.

Example 2.15 shows a similar case of N turning a strong statement against the negotiation ("I wanna die today.", lines 05–06) to a topic in PiC's domain. Here, N1 has just arrived at the scene and asks PiC for an update: "what is it you want to do" (lines 02–03).

```
Example 2.15: Today is the day for me
01   N:     Oliver I t- I turned up a little
02          bit late.=I know so.hh what- what
03          is it you want to do.
04              (2.1)
05   PiC:   I wanna (t-/d-) (0.4) I wanna
06          die today.
07              (0.8)
08   PiC:   Today. Is the day for me.
09              (0.6)
```

From all possible answers to "what is it that you want to do", an answer that says the recipient wants to end life is pretty serious. Classic conversation analytic research on suicide helplines has shown how suicidal people struggle with people in their everyday life, not taking their suicidal thoughts or threats seriously and laughing it off (Sacks, 1992). Helpline professionals should take the threat seriously, and so should crisis negotiators. How do they take the threat seriously? In Example 2.15, the negotiator does not laugh, dismiss PiC's threat, or challenge the legitimacy. N does not ask, "why would you do that?", which would be a way to distance oneself from the act of suicide or its legitimacy. Instead N acknowledges PiC's decision by asking him "why today" (line 10).

```
Example 2.15: Today is the day for me (cont'd)
09              (0.6)
10   N:     Wh- why to[day.  ]
11   PiC:              [Today]: is the day
12          for ~me~.
13              (0.4)
14   N:     Wh- why why sp-
15          spe[cifically >today<.]
16   PiC:      [Today is the day ] for me (though).
```

Asking, "why today" sounds the exact opposite of asking, "why at all". The question does not challenge PiC's decision, but instead challenges the decision to do it "now". There are fundamental reasons why we point out the distinction of word choice, which we will return to later in this book. Next, let us see how N pursues an answer to his question: PiC does not immediately answer to the "why", but instead persists on his decision to do it. N pursues his question in line 10, then again in lines 14–15 and line 18, before PiC starts his expanded answer in line 20.

```
Example 2.15: Today is the day for me (cont'd)
17              (0.7)
18   N:     But why's that Oliver.
19              (3.0)
20   N:     What's particularly happened
21          today to (0.5) to make you
22          wanna die today.
23              (1.0)
24   PiC:   There's been an ongoing situation.
25              (0.6)
26   PiC:   And ongoing.
```

```
27                    (.)
28   PiC:    And ongoing.
29                    (0.7)
30   PiC:    That's why I've been takin' (0.4)
31           all these medication: (.) been
32           (0.2) fucking in and out (.) of
33           hospital _
34                    (1.0)
35   PiC:    It's been an ongoing situation.
```

In each of his turns of talk, N pursues the topic initially put forward by the question "why today". In lines 20–22 he reformulates his pursuit of an answer with "what's particularly happened... to make you wanna die today", effectively spelling out to PiC what was meant by his initial "why" question.

These are concrete examples of the non-judgmental approach to negotiation promoted elsewhere in the training literature (McMains & Mullins, 2014). While some training recommends avoiding "why" questions (e.g., James, 2008), our research points to examples of how "why" questions work in sequences of real crisis negotiations, which are essential to getting the conversation started.

LESSONS ON HOW TO GET PAST EARLY RESISTANCE

- Faced with strong resistance, questions such as "what happened (today)" are more effective than offers to help/talk to get beyond the opening and starting a first topic of conversation.
- Effective questions address knowledge within the person in crisis's domain, and do not directly threaten the person in crisis's choices or decisions.

We will return to the power of questions later in the book, also on the popular distinction between open/closed-ended questions. As a note of caution, the distinction between open/closed-ended questions is not as clear-cut as it seems at first. While readers may agree the effective questions reported in this chapter fall under the 'open-ended' category, there are plenty of examples where closed-ended questions (yes/no interrogatives) effectively get topics and negotiation processes moving. We return to such examples throughout the book, and further address this point in Chapter 8.

SUMMARY

In this chapter we have shown how crisis negotiators get past first introductions and early resistance. To better understand the particular challenges crisis negotiators face, we compared openings of crisis encounters with other kinds of encounters. Compared to most interactional contexts, we have seen how crisis negotiations are characterized by strong resistance, and that this resistance is evident from the very first turn of talk.

TAKEAWAY PRACTICAL STRATEGIES: OPENING A NEGOTIATION

- Make it known you're with the police to get beyond the opening introductions. There is no benefit in hiding your association with the police.

- Questions about "what's happening", and "why today" are useful because they put the person in crisis in the position of knowing, without being threatened.

- Questions like "Tell me what happened (today)" are more effective than assurances that "I'd (really) like to help you" to get the conversation started. That is because questions can be pursued and reformulated, whereas offers of 'help' leave the way open for reasons not to engage.

- As long as questions are in the persons in crisis's domain (something only they can know), and do not threaten their choices (e.g., to be on a roof), it is less important whether or not they are open-ended. In fact, most 'closed-ended' questions (including yes/no interrogatives) are more open than you think. The 'open' versus 'closed' questions distinction is partly a myth, which we unpack further in Chapter 8.

Getting the conversation started

In our research we have found that negotiators deal with these challenges by (i) introducing themselves with reference to affiliation ("I'm with the police"), and (ii) asking first questions whose answers are in the persons in crisis's domain and which do not threaten their choice, including "why today?" and "what happened?". These are some of the ways negotiators get the conversation going and prevent hang-ups or other forms of disengagement.

REFERENCES

Clayman, S. E., & Heritage, J. (2002). Questioning presidents: Journalistic deference and adversarialness in the press conferences of US Presidents Eisenhower and Reagan. *Journal of Communication, 52*(4), 749–775.

Heritage, J. (1984). A change-of-state token and aspects of its sequential placement. In Atkinson, J.M, & Heritage, J. (Eds.), *Structures of social action: Studies in conversation analysis* (pp. 299–345). Cambridge, UK: Cambridge University Press.

James, R. K. (2008). *Crisis intervention strategies*. Belmont, CA: Thomson Brooks/ Cole.

McMains, M., & Mullins, W. C. (2014). *Crisis negotiations: Managing critical incidents and hostage situations in law enforcement and corrections*. New York: Routledge.

Miller, L. (2005). Hostage negotiation: Psychological principles and practices. *International Journal of Emergency Mental Health, 7*(4), 277.

Roberts, A. R. (Ed.). (2005). *Crisis intervention handbook: Assessment, treatment, and research*. New York: Oxford University Press.

Sacks, H. (1992). *Lectures on conversation* [1964–1972]. Oxford: Blackwell.

Schegloff, E. A. (1968). Sequencing in conversational openings. *American Anthropologist, 70*(6), 1075–1095.

Stokoe, E. (2018). *Talk: The science of conversation*. London: Hachette UK.

Strentz, T. (2018). *Psychological aspects of crisis negotiation*. New York: Routledge.

How words reduce resistance towards the negotiation

Chapter 3

DOI: 10.4324/9780429354892-3

WHAT IS THIS CHAPTER ABOUT?

Despite the best of intentions, negotiators may say something that a person in crisis can then use as the basis for resistance or to close the conversation. Such resistance makes for unproductive negotiations, by generating the need to overcome it and, each time this happens, further extending the encounter. In this chapter, we show how the risk of a hang-up, and other strong forms of resistance, including disengagement and escalation, may increase or decrease depending on the words negotiators use, as well as how negotiators mitigate the risk through selecting other words. Specifically, we show how offers to 'help' and 'talk' are not productive for the negotiation and may indeed be counter-productive.

First, we show that the word 'help', which is commonly formulated into an offer at the start of negotiations, is frequently resisted by persons in crisis, and generates a hurdle which must then be overcome. Second, we show how 'help' and 'talk' are more readily rejected than comparable formulations (including synonyms), in terms of the difference made for the ensuing conversation. We also show how initial resistance can open up opportunities to engage rather than disengage the person in crisis. Finally, we show the alternative and more productive words and resources available for progressing the negotiation past early resistance.

We ask:

How may the negotiator's choice of words influence engagement from the person in crisis?

WHY IS THIS AN IMPORTANT TOPIC?

One of the ways that essence of crisis negotiation is articulated is through the verb 'to talk'. Indeed, the strapline for the New York Police Department's service is 'talk to me' (see Bråten et al. 2016) . The phrase 'talk to me' captures the principle that talking, that is, negotiating, is a solution to the crisis, which is not built on coercion but rather on verbal strategies allowing the person in crisis to vent their feelings and resolve the confrontations over time (Van Hasselt et al., 2006). 'Talk to me' techniques favour a 'soft' as opposed to 'hard' negotiation approach. But what happens when negotiators present their intentions to 'talk' to persons in crisis? Do negotiators do so explicitly, using this or other words? How does a person in crisis respond to a negotiator's voiced commitment to 'talk' as the means to a solution? Can a single word change the outcome of an interaction?

In this chapter, we will see how words associated with formulating the negotiator's purpose tend to be the same words that people in crisis use to reject the negotiation. That is, persons in crisis treat police formulations such as "I'm here to help", "can we talk?", and "because I care about you" as explicit resources to reject the negotiation. This chapter demonstrates the critical relevance of word choice; specifically, how rejections from persons in crisis affect how negotiators formulate their turns at talk. Not only does every *turn* of talk matter, but every *word* also matters.

WHAT CURRENT TRAINING TELLS US ABOUT WORD CHOICE

Crisis negotiators may be aware there is no 'magic wand' to resolving the crisis: no single word or formulation will make a person who's barricaded themselves to move to safety. Instead, according to existing approaches, a successful negotiation moves slowly, allowing for the person in crisis to decide to move to safety. Meanwhile, some negotiator moves are more likely to lead to resistance than others. What are those moves, and how does one craft them? These are empirical questions that guide this book and this chapter.

Regarding word choice, the literature uses the principle of active listening skills (ALS) as a starting point (see e.g., Vecchi, Van Hasselt, & Romano, 2005). For example, regarding the goal of showing empathy, negotiators are trained to mirror the person in crisis and employ emotional labelling such as, "That must have been hard/sad/frightening", or "I can hear you're angry." Another principle in ALS is 'I' messages, like "I feel uneasy when you talk like that." These statements show the negotiator's concern and provide an account for that concern (see also McMains & Mullins, 2014, for an overview). In addition to 'talk to me' as a frequently used motto, James (2008) introduces the

How words reduce resistance

notion 'facilitative listening', suggesting particular formats for requesting dialogue: "Please tell me...", "Show me...", "In what ways does...?"; to focus on the future, and "What will you do...". James (2008) also provides more extended examples of 'facilitative listening.' For example (p. 56):

> Rita, I can see you're really hurting. To fully understand what's going on and what needs to be done, I'm going to focus as hard as I can on what you're saying and how you're saying it. As well as listening to what you do say, I'm going to be listening for those things that aren't said because they may have some bearing on your problems too. So, if I seem to be really concentrating on you, it's because I want to fully comprehend in as helpful and objective a way as possible what the situation is and your readiness to do something about it.

Because this is presented as a verbatim transcript, we do not know if there are opportunities for the person in crisis to respond at any point in what appears to be a monologue. Without information about the placement, timing, and delivery of the exemplar interaction above, it is not easy to assess the transcript and understand it; for example, when and where the person in crisis *could* answer, and if so, what they would say. Existing training typically does not demonstrate actual opportunities for the person in crisis to engage in the interaction.

Some notion of 'help' is core to how we describe the need for someone in crisis and what professionals can offer; indeed, suicidal persons are classically characterised as making a "cry for help" (e.g., Farberow & Shneidman, 1961) while research also shows that this is not how survivors necessarily account for their actions (e.g., Maple et al., 2019).

While institutionalized help is available in helplines and therapy and can potentially work to prevent suicide (Rosenberg et al., 1989; see also Baker, Emmison, & Firth, 2005 for an overview on helpline services), not all suicidal people in crisis seek professional assistance as a first step. Resistance to seeking help in the first place is a common topic in the psychological literature on suicide prevention, specifically on how suicidal individuals may negate, refuse, or avoid seeking help. Resisting help is referred to as the 'help negation effect' (Clark & Fawcett, 1992; Gould et al., 2012;). Importantly, individuals in crisis have not sought help; negotiators are accountable for approaching *them*. This has consequences for the interaction and, as we will show, also has consequences for how people in crisis respond to offers of 'help', and 'talk'.

HOW PURSUING 'HELP' AS THE SOLUTION TO THE CRISIS IS COUNTER-PRODUCTIVE

In Chapter 2, we saw how negotiators come to formulate their purpose using the verbs 'help' and 'talk.'. We found that negotiators refer to 'help' and 'talk' when they first account for their presence in the encounter's opening as they emerge at the scene. We demonstrated how negotiators observably do so to distance themselves from other police. While negotiators promote 'help' and 'talk' as the primary purpose, persons in crisis often resist or reject them. Examples 3.1 and 3.2 are two cases in point. In Example 3.1, N has just arrived inside a building where PiC is barricaded inside her flat, visible to N through a locked gate-like door.

```
Example 3.1:  I'm dying tonight
01     N:         [...] my job is to sit here
02               and talk to you and try and help.
03                    (0.4)
04     N:         See what we can do to help ya.
05                    (0.5)
06     PiC:       You ca:n't. I'm dying tonight
07                (real soon).
```

In line 01 N formulates the purpose ('help') and method ('talk') of the negotiation: "my job is to sit here and talk to you and try and help.". Following a gap, N reformulates the purpose as an explorative process ("See what we can do"). In line 06 PiC rejects N's proposal outright: "You ca:n't", followed by the account "I'm dying tonight...", which not only claims a decision to end her life but that the end is imminent, using the present continuous form of the verb 'dying'. We find this a recurrent event: people in crisis position their intentions in perfect opposition to the negotiator proposal, and offer an absolute 'no', in this case "You ca:n't" [help me].

Example 3.2 represents a similar type of rejection. PiC is barricaded in his flat and the negotiators have established contact with PiC via his telephone number. PiC keeps hanging up the telephone as the negotiators are reluctant to give PiC cigarettes he demands unless he talks to them.

```
Example 3.2: There's nothing you can do
01   N:      I just want to help
02           [you out.            ]
03   PiC:    [There's- there's] there's n:othing
04           you can do::.
```

Here N offers "to help" and yet PiC rejects this offer. Before this exchange, PiC has already indicated resistance to engaging in dialogue: as in Example 3.1 the "just" in "I just want to help you out." (line 01) seems to deal with such resistance, framing *help* as something quite the opposite of putting demands on PiC, not representing any invasive agenda. But in his response, PiC shows that 'help' is anything but acceptable: "There's n:othing you can do::", with marked prominence on "nothing", rejects N's offer outright. By rejecting N's offer in this way, PiC treats it as irrelevant and categorically so. That is, whatever 'help' represents, it will not meet PiC's needs. Also, the format of PiC's rejection, and its placement, make it clear that there is no reason to specify further what 'help' might look like. PiC's rejection ("There's-there's") immediately follows N's production of the word "help". PiC keeps talking through N's further production of his turn, thereby treating N's further talk – and any possible unpacking of what "help" might mean – as inconsequential to his answer.

In both Examples 3.1 and 3.2, PiC rejects outright N's intentions. In the next few examples, we will see exactly how promoting 'help' is counter-productive for the negotiation.

In Example 3.3, N has made contact with PiC on the telephone. PiC is barricaded in his flat, threatening to shoot either himself or the police should they try to enter. Early in the call, N proposes that PiC might want to "talk to me for a bit?" (line 01) to "try and help ya," (lines 02–03).

```
Example 3.3: Everyone is worried about you
01   N:      Do you wanna talk to me for a bit?
02           I mean (uh-) (.) I am gonna try
03           and help ya,
04                   (1.5)
05   PiC:    (       )=
06   N:      =I- I wanted t- I sort of like
07           want to try and get to the
08           bottom of this.=An:.hhh everyone
09           out here is sort of like really
10           worried about ya.
11                   (0.4)
```

Following a 1.5 second gap (line 04), PiC produces some inaudible response, and N further unpacks her purpose in lines 06–10: "get to the bottom of this" then points to 'the problem', the helpable matter, without specifying any further what this might be. N proceeds to generalize her concern with "everyone out here is [...] worried about ya." (lines 08–10). What is evident in this case is the absence of an acceptance from PiC to N's offer to help. Across cases, we find that negotiators offering to help by generalizing their concern (e.g. that "everyone is worried about you") is not productive in terms of getting PiC on board with the offer.

Overall, we find that negotiators struggle to pursue 'help' early on in the encounter. Example 3.4 presents a case. Here the negotiator attempts to pursue 'help' with a question which, instead of clarifying the need for help, highlights the problem of offering it without a concrete way of understanding what 'help' means for PiC.

```
Example 3.4: How CAN we help you
01   N:      That's exactly why I'm here.
```

How words reduce resistance

02		Just to see if we can he̲lp,
03		(1.6)
04	N:	But how ca̲n we help you Oliver,
05		(5.2)

In this case, PiC challenges N as to their purpose and role as negotiator, which PiC treats as incompatible with N's formulation of purpose. In line 01, N reiterates their point that negotiators' role is "just to see if we can help,". This does not lead to any verbal acknowledgment from PiC. Following a 1.6 second gap, N continues with "But how ca̲n we help you" (line 04). Formulated as an interrogative, the negotiator himself questions the relevance or applicability of 'help'. This highlights the problem with 'help' to start with: it has not been sought and is not (yet) specified. It stands in marked contrast, both in design and placement, to standard service openers "how can I help": the phrasal prominence is on *can*, turning this into a rhetorical question rather than something N actually expects an answer to. And PiC is in no hurry to answer: the negotiator's question is followed by a 5.2 second gap of silence. While there is no explicit rejection of 'help' in Examples 3.3 and 3.4, PiC is not treating *help* as relevant or specific enough.

LESSONS LEARNED FROM EXAMPLES 3.1–3.4

- General offers of 'help' are not treated positively by persons in crisis, and such offers, once made, create barriers in the negotiation, as evidenced by how negotiators struggle to unpack what 'help' might mean specifically to the person in crisis.
- We did not find examples where a proposal to 'help' is followed by a person in crisis moving towards agreement or collaboration in the next turn.
- We did not find instances of the person in crisis asking for 'help' proactively.

In the next section we show that, as with proposals to 'help', people in crisis reject proposals to 'talk' by contrasting them with specific, purposeful actions.

EXPLICIT RESISTANCE TO 'TALK' (AND 'HELP') AS THE SOLUTION TO THE CRISIS

When negotiators propose dialogue, they frequently use the verb 'talk'. However, we found that, for people in crisis, the verb 'talk' made it easier to reject dialogue altogether, and thus the negotiation process, than alternative verbs that also describe dialogue. We return to alternatives to 'talk' and 'help' later in the chapter (don't look yet!) and show how these alternatives are less prone to explicit resistance and rejection.

Example 3.5 provides a clear case of a PiC rejecting a N's request to 'talk'. PiC contrasts 'talk' with his own agenda, thereby undermining its relevance. Prior to this excerpt, PiC has demanded cigarettes.

```
Example 3.5: I don't want to talk
01   N:     Kevin, I need to:: try and find
02          a way. to get you those cigarettes.=
03          =In the meantim:e,
04          Can we talk about how you are.
05                 (0.5)
06   PiC:   No:, I don't want to ta:lk,
07                 (1.0)
08   PiC:   Y[ou either] ↑ring me when you've
09   N:      [°Okay°    ]
10   PiC:   got the fucking cigarettes or
11          don't bother.
12                 (0.2)
13   N:     (m)kay,=What's what's going to
14          happen when we get the cigarettes
15          though Kevin.
16                    (0.6) / ((PiC hangs up))
```

N uses PiC's demand as part of an offer in lines 01–04: "I need to:: try and find a way. to get you those cigarettes." but defers delivery of the cigarettes and makes a proposal to talk "In the meantime" (line 03). N's proposal is rejected outright, with a prolonged "No:,", followed by an affirmation of the rejection in a full clausal form: "I don't want to talk" (line 06). PiC does not explicitly account for his rejection, but instead displays a negative stance towards 'talk' via the way he over-pronounces the word. In non-technical terms, it sounds as though the word 'talk' is delivered with scare quotes around it.

Example 3.5 shows how a person in crisis orients explicitly to the word 'talk' itself, and the activity it proposes, as problematic. PiC not only emphasizes the activity he rejects but repeats it in a way which accentuates how far he is from accepting N's proposal, treating 'talk' as irrelevant. Next, PiC produces an ultimatum in either-or format ("You either ↑ring me when you've the fucking cigarettes or don't bother.", lines 08/10–11). While the ultimatum does not include a time limit (hence, no urgency), it conveys his intention to reject dialogue until his side of the deal is fulfilled. In lines 13–15, N expresses his concern that nothing might happen after they give PiC the cigarettes. PiC hangs up (line 16).

Following PiC's hang up in Example 3.5, the negotiators attempt a next phone call to the same PiC in Example 3.6. Here we find N acknowledging a prior response about PiC's complaint regarding the police officer "Kevin" (line 01). In a next move N praises PiC for "starting to talk' (line 03), which for N is the relevant, and primary focal activity. However, notice how easily PiC explicitly rejects 'talk' by contrasting it with having already told N what he wanted to say.

```
Example 3.6: I've no need to talk about it
01   N:      >Okay well< we can talk about that
02           Kevin, That's good.=
03   N:      =[I'm glad- I'm glad you're starting to]=
04   PiC:    =[I've no need to talk about it,=I've]=
05   N:      =[talk.=.hhhh    ]
06   PiC:    =[just told you] what he's doing,
```

Another observation includes how N displays appreciation of talk, "That's good.", first in line 02 then expanded in line 03. In overlap with N (line 04), PiC rejects the relevance of 'talk' and any positive connotations with the activity 'talk' represents. By proceeding in overlap, N maintains the relevance of 'talk' while PiC rejects it.

We found that negotiators do, on occasion, explicitly formulate why talking is worth doing. However, people in crisis do not do so, and they do not affiliate with positive evaluations of 'talk'. Instead, they build upon positive reasons for talking, as provided by negotiators, to articulate their 'way out' of the conversation. Example 3.7 further demonstrates this point.

```
Example 3.7: Talking costs nothing
01   N:     Let's just carry on talking for a while.
02               (0.6)
03   N:     (cal-) talking costs nothing does it.
04               (1.3)
05   PiC:   Yeah it does,=It costs me time,
06               (0.6)
```

Following the inter-turn gap in line 02, N pursues an acceptance of his dialogue proposal in line 01, with a declarative assertion "talking costs nothing", followed by the tag question format "does it.". These types of tag questions set up expectations for an agreement – in this case that "talking costs nothing". However, PiC does not agree. Following a 1.3 second gap, she disagrees with N's assertion on the basis that "It costs me time," (line 05). PiC thereby rejects the dialogue proposal, by flipping N's attempt to frame 'talk' as low in cost for her own purposes.

Why is it that when negotiators provide positive evaluations of 'talk' as part of proposing dialogue, PiC rejects the proposal as well as N's positive evaluation in explicit terms? One explanation comes from how, across cultures, 'talk' is the subject of hundreds of idioms and proverbs: we "talk the talk", "talk is cheap", and we "talk a mile a minute". To "talk the talk"', first used in 1906, is usually contrasted with "to walk the walk".

How words reduce resistance

The words of someone who "talks the talk" are just rhetoric and without substance; someone who "walks the walk" supports their rhetoric with action. Likewise, the American proverb, "talk is cheap" is "used for saying that you do not believe that someone will in fact do what they are saying they will do."[1] There are no related idioms in English containing 'speak'.

This idiomatic use of 'talk' is evident in our research. In Example 3.8, PiC uses 'talk' to actively undermine dialogue, and the negotiation, having just rejected a proposal put forward by N to solve the crisis. PiC contrasts 'talk' with specific, purposeful actions. The negotiator suggests that the mental health charity, 'Mind', might be able to help PiC.

```
Example 3.8: Have you heard of Mind
01   N:      I'll tell you what we can get at the
02           police station.=We can get. (0.4)
03           a m- a mental health charity,=Have you
04           heard of Mi:nd at all?
05                   (1.9)
06   PiC:    Say that again,
07   N:      Have you heard of Mi:nd,
08                   (3.0)
09   PiC:    I've seen a poster >on the bus<.=
10   N:      =Yeah?=An' (another) ano-.hh an:'-.h
11           you know..hh the local poli:ce,  (.)
12           can get those people.h to
13           come to the police station,
14                   (2.0)
15   N:      And that's g- that's >there you go<,
16           That's a starter for ten isn't it.
17                   (0.4)
18   PiC:    °Yes (but) ( )°
19                   (0.4)
20   N:      You know. [uh- ]
21   PiC:             [(no) ]
```

```
22              (.)
23    N:    And that- that you know that's help
24          we can you know (.) genuinely provide.
25          We could get them there (in the-)
26          .h you know tomorrow morning.
27    PiC:  That's not help.
28                  (.)
29    PiC:  What- i:- that's not help.=i- that's
30          not: (0.4) <that's not uh::m:>
31          getting me a place.
32                  (1.0)
33    PiC:  That's just the police who's talking.
34                  (2.5)
35    PiC:  It's all talking now.
```

The example starts about 90 minutes into the negotiation. PiC has resisted N's proposal to come down and accompany him to the police station. PiC has previously been involved with social services but has now turned 18 and is ineligible for support. He is also concerned that his situation will worsen if he goes to the police station. In lines 01–04, N specifies alternative support with the mental health charity 'Mind'. N does so in a longer turn: "I'll tell you what we can get" (line 01) sets the frame for additional turn components to specify the proposed solution. Before any change of speaker, N requests a confirmation whether PiC has heard of 'Mind' ("Have you heard of Mi:nd at all?", line 04), in which the "at all" opens for a "no" as a relevant response, i.e., opening for the possibility that PiC has not heard of this charity. Following a 1.9 second gap (line 05), PiC initiates a repair in line 06 ("Say that again,"), which, compared to the strong forms of resistance we saw in some of the earlier cases, aligns with rather than prevents N from progressing his proposal.

We observe that PiC gives the go-ahead to N's solution-based proposal ("I've seen a poster >on the bus<.", line 09), which N then proceeds to unpack in lines 10–16. PiC then displays weaker forms of resistance in lines 18–20, before N formulates

How words reduce resistance

the proposed alternative as "help we can you know (.) genuinely provide." (lines 23–24). PiC now rejects N outright, with "That's not help." (line 27), using N's very own formulation "help". With this move, PiC also rejects the possibility of seeing the charity, "tomorrow morning", as N suggests in line 26. PiC accounts for his rejection of N's proposed solution in lines 29–35, first explaining how going to the police station and meeting the charity is not "getting [PiC] a place." (line 31; PiC here refers to his previously expressed wishes to leave his home and his abusive mother to get his own place to live). Then, PiC adds to his account with the use of "talk" in lines 33 ("That's just the police who's talking.") and 35 ("It's all talking now."). Thus, PiC treats N's proposed solution (i.e., 'help') as not doing anything relevant or useful. This fits with the idiomatic use of 'talk' as 'not action': we observe that when specific actions are offered, the verb 'talk' is a resource to reject the offer, highlighted as contrasting with actual help.

LESSONS LEARNED FROM EXAMPLES 3.5–3.8

- When specific actions are offered, 'help' and 'talk' are resources to reject the offer, highlighted as contrasting with actual help.

- It is with 'help' and 'talk' that a person in crisis turns from engaging in the conversation to undermining it.

- Based on this analysis we argue that 'help' and 'talk' open slots for resistance, however they can be avoided: next, we demonstrate that such rejections are less explicit when alternatives to 'talk' and 'help' are used, i.e. 'sort' and 'speak'.

HOW 'SORT(ING OUT X)' IS HARDER TO REJECT THAN 'HELP'

Having identified the challenges with pursuing and highlighting 'help' and 'talk', we now turn our attention to alternative ways of proposing help. Naturally, negotiators do not propose a concrete resolution until they have gathered intelligence about the person in crisis's situation. Thus, resistance to the negotiation seems based on lack of evidence that the negotiator can help. For someone prone to resist the negotiation, such lacking evidence can further fuel the reasoning behind their resistance. However, where offers to help are met with rejection based on lack of evidence, PiCs are less likely to reject an offer when negotiators frame an activity as "sort out X", even early on in the negotiation.

To 'sort' opens for a more concrete outcome than 'help', and this is based on the grammar. Whereas 'help' does not require an object, 'sort' does: there's a missing X in a sentence starting with "I can sort out...". Or when formulated as "I can sort IT out", the "it" refers to something specific, or at least the person who says it is accountable for defining what "it" is. In Example 3.9, PiC seeks to unpack exactly how the negotiator suggests to "sort that out". In this encounter, PiC has been involved with social services previously, on account of his abusive mother and mental health problems. PiC, now having turned 18, does not have the same access to social services, and the negotiator proposes that different mental health charities can provide support. Following N's promise to "sort out" any related problems with PiC's mother (lines 11–13), PiC asks, "So if I go to the station what happens then." (lines 17–18). In this way, PiC is not rejecting N's promise to "sort X out", but invites N to elaborate exactly how.

```
Example 3.9: Get it sorted out
01  N:    This is what I'm saying.=This is why
02        we've got to go down the police station
03        and get it sorted ou:t.
04                (0.8)
05  N:    So that we can get (.).h doctors,
06        We can get (.).h you know..hh
07        mental health charities, We can get
08        local >authority<,=All to sta:rt¿
09        .h giving you a leg up.
10                (1.2)
11  N:    Okay,=And also when we can sort out=
12        .hh you know if your mum's making
13        up storie:s,.h then we can sort that out.
14                (0.3)
```

How words reduce resistance

```
15   N:     Okay?
16                 (.)
17   PiC:   So if I go to the station what
18          happens then.
```

Although formulations of how a problem can be "sorted out" typically occur much later in the crisis negotiations, there are some cases where solutions are proposed at the very outset of the encounter. Example 3.10 is taken from early on in an encounter where N contacts PiC over the phone. N does not formulate purpose as 'help', but as already having some idea that something needs sorting out. N proposes that she "come down" and "speak to you" (lines 02–03), meaning that she proposes she comes within audible range to PiC to continue the conversation from his building. In this way, the negotiator suggests dialogue with a purpose without using the verbs 'talk' and 'help'.

```
Example 3.10: Miss I'm so scared
01   N:     Eh y- and an'(uh) I d- you know. (.)
02          And I wanna get- and I wanna come down
03          and I wanna speak to you..hhh
04          [and see if we can sort this out.]
05   PiC:   [Miss. I'm so scared.            ]=
06          I stabbed myself in the neck.
07   PiC:   #(And I[:)# ]
08   N:            [I kn]o::w.
09   N:     .hh I know. You must've been
10          so frightened,
```

Example 3.10 happens approximately 2 minutes into the encounter. N offers to "come down and I wanna speak to you. .hhh and see if we can sort this out." (lines 01–04). PiC affiliates with N, admitting to being in some distress (line 05), and referring to a past incident of having stabbed himself (lines 05–06).

What can we learn from these examples? That offers to resolve a problem are successful when tied to concrete actions, and that 'sort' is more closely tied to such concrete actions than 'help', as is evident from how negotiators use these words, and people in crisis's responses to them.

HOW 'SPEAK' IS HARDER TO REJECT THAN 'TALK'

We found that when negotiators propose dialogue using the word 'speak' they are not met by similar strong forms of resistance forms as when proposing dialogue using the word 'talk'. PiCs do not highlight 'speak' (and 'sort') as irrelevant or something they explicitly do not want to engage with. The evidence that 'speak' is less prone to resistance than 'talk' is both quantitative and qualitative: there are no cases in the data where the verb 'speak' is used to resist the ongoing activity, such as "I don't want to speak", "this is all speaking now", "speaking isn't doing anything" – all uses we do find with the verb 'talk'.

Overall, proposals to 'speak' are less likely to be faced with explicit rejections. We find more examples of some form of an agreement following 'speak': these findings are summarised in Figure 3.1 (see also Sikveland & Stokoe, 2020).

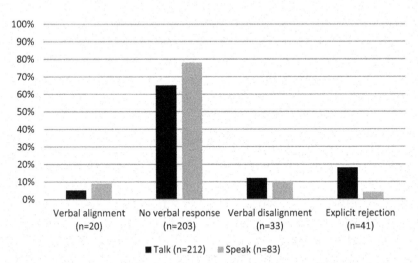

Figure 3.1 Distribution of second pair part response types following negotiators' dialogue proposal, to 'talk' (black) or 'speak' (light grey). Each proportional value is normalized according to respective total 'talk' (n=212) and 'speak' (n=83) proposals. Total n=295 and proportions exclude cases where both verbs are used within the same turn.

Returning to Example 3.10, now 3.11 for this next example, the negotiator expresses her intention to come and 'speak' to PiC. N's proposal to 'speak' gets associated with their promise to "sort this out".

```
Example 3.11: Miss I'm so scared
01   N:        Eh y- and an'(uh) I d- you know.
02              (.) And I wanna get- and I wanna
03              come down and I wanna speak to you..hhh
04              [and see if we can sort this out.]
05   PiC:       [Miss. I'm so scared.              ]=
06              I stabbed myself in the neck.
07   PiC:       #(And I[:)#  ]
08   N:                 [I kn]o::w.
09   N:        .hh I know. You must've been
10              so frightened,
```

As N proposes dialogue, PiC responds with expressed affiliation with the negotiator's concern in lines 05–06: "I'm so scared. I stabbed myself in the neck", referring to an earlier incident. The response opens an opportunity for N to show her concern, which she does in lines 09–10: "You must've been so frightened,". This productive exchange happens after N proposes dialogue with 'speak'. Our analyses show that PiCs may go along with dialogue proposals to 'speak', especially when associated with concrete outcomes.

When people in crisis resist dialogue proposals to 'speak', they do so in implicit and not in explicit terms. In Example 3.12, the person in crisis is not rejecting the dialogue proposal with 'speak' in explicit terms and invites the negotiator to elaborate rather than closing down opportunities for sequential progression.

```
Example 3.12: What for?
01    N:        One- once you've got them.=Will you
02              speak to me then.
03                    (2.0)
```

```
04   N:        So we could try and [work:-   ]
05   PiC:                          [↑What fo]:r.
06              (0.3)
07   N:        So we can work through a way to
08             help you.
```

Finally, people in crisis never ask to "talk to" a negotiator in our data. They may ask to "talk to" a third party, like a parent or someone they interacted with earlier, however, 'speak' is more frequently associated with such more future activities.

```
Example 3.13: I want to speak to her
01   N:     You said for the sake of your children.=
02          Why don't you come down for them.
03   PiC:   I've already spoke. I'm spea- I wanna
04          speak to her.
05              (.)
06   PiC:   Not you.
07              (.)
08   N:     You want to speak to who:?
09              (0.9)
10   PiC:   THAT police officer.
```

LESSONS LEARNED FROM EXAMPLES 3.9–3.13

- It is easier to reject proposals to 'help', than to 'sort' (out X).
- It is easier to reject dialogue proposals to 'talk', than to 'speak'.
- Changing from one word to another can reduce the amount and extent of resistance in the negotiation.
- While crisis negotiations are filled with resistance, some actions, and words, are easier to resist than others and careful analysis can reveal what they are.

SUMMARY

In this chapter, we have shown how engagement, or rather, the extent to which a person in crisis resists and rejects the negotiation, is closely tied to word choice. We have focussed on the use of 'help' and 'talk'. Our research shows that persons in crisis treat formulations such as "I'm here to help", "can we talk?", and "because I care about you" as explicit resources to reject the negotiation: possibly because the person in crisis has experienced similar situations, and promises, in the past. The verbs 'help' and 'talk' are thus unhelpful and counter-productive in contrast to perhaps more instrumental-sounding verbs, such as 'sort' and 'speak' (or 'deal' as opposed to 'care'; see also Sikveland & Stokoe, 2020). The person in crisis resists offers of 'help' and 'talk' when couched *as* help and talk, which does not happen following proposals to 'sort' or 'speak'. These findings suggest how negotiators may choose words strategically to convey commitment and credibility: 'actions, not words'.

TAKEAWAY PRACTICAL STRATEGIES: HOW WORD CHOICE INCREASES OR REDUCES RESISTANCE

- To minimize resistance towards dialogue, try proposing dialogue with 'speak' rather than 'talk'. 'Speak' is harder to reject than 'talk', partly because it is less tied to idiomatic forms like "it's just talk", and "talk = no action".

- To offer support, work towards proposing something specific, with 'sort' rather than 'help'. Explicit offers to 'help' are a difficult sell for individuals who have not asked for it.

NOTE

1 The earliest date for publication of the phrase "talk is cheap" is found in the Chicago Daily Tribune on November 21, 1891. https://idiomation.wordpress.com/

REFERENCES

Baker, C., Emmison, M., & Firth, A. (Eds.). (2005). *Calling for help: Language and social interaction in telephone helplines* (Vol. 143). Amsterdam: John Benjamins Publishing.

Bråten, O. A., St-Yves, M., Royce, Terry, D., & Laforest, M. (2016). Hostage and crisis negotiation, perspectives on an interactive process. In Oxburgh, G., Myklebust,

T., Grant, T., & Milne, R. (Eds.) *Communication in investigative and legal contexts: Integrated approaches from forensic psychology, linguistics and law enforcement* (s. 231–257). Chichester: John Wiley & Sons.

Clark, D. C., & Fawcett, J. (1992). Review of empirical risk factors for evaluation of the suicidal patient. In Bongar, B. M. (Ed.), *Suicide: Guidelines for assessment, management, and treatment* (pp. 16–48). New York: Oxford University Press.

Farberow, N. L., & Shneidman, E. S. (Eds.). (1961). *The cry for help*. New York: McGraw-Hill.

Gould, M. S., Munfakh, J. L., Kleinman, M., & Lake, A. M. (2012). National suicide prevention lifeline: enhancing mental health care for suicidal individuals and other people in crisis. *Suicide and Life-Threatening Behavior, 42*(1), 22–35.

James, R. K. (2008). *Crisis intervention strategies*. Belmont, CA: Thomson Brooks/ Cole.

Maple, M., Frey, L. M., McKay, K., Coker, S., & Grey, S. (2019). "Nobody Hears a Silent Cry for Help": Suicide Attempt Survivors' Experiences of Disclosing During and After a Crisis. *Archives of Suicide Research*, 1–19.

McMains, M., & Mullins, W. C. (2014). *Crisis negotiations: Managing critical incidents and hostage situations in law enforcement and corrections*. New York: Routledge.

Pudlinski, C. (2005). Doing empathy and sympathy: Caring responses to troubles tellings on a peer support line. *Discourse Studies, 7*(3), 267–288.

Rosenberg, M. L., Eddy, D. M., Wolpert, R. C., & Broumas, E. P. (1989). Developing strategies to prevent youth suicide. In Pfeffer, C. R. (Ed.) *Suicide among youth: Perspectives on risk and prevention* (203–225). Washington, DC: American Psychiatric Press.

Sikveland, R. O., & Stokoe, E. (2020). Should police negotiators ask to "talk" or "speak" to persons in crisis? Word selection and overcoming resistance to dialogue proposals. *Research on Language and Social Interaction, 53*(3), 324–340.

Vecchi, G.M., Van Hasselt, V.B., & Romano, S.S. (2005). Crisis (hostage) negotiation: Current strategies and issues in high-risk conflict resolution, *Aggression and Violent Behaviour, 10*, 533–551.

Van Hasselt, V. B., Baker, M. T., Romano, S. J., Schlessinger, K. M., Zucker, M., Dragone, R., & Perera, A. L. (2006). Crisis (hostage) negotiation training: A preliminary evaluation of program efficacy. *Criminal Justice and Behavior, 33*(1), 56–69.

Managing emotion

Chapter 4

WHAT IS THIS CHAPTER ABOUT?

In this chapter, we show how negotiators and other professionals
deal with the strong emotions expressed by persons in crisis
in order to de-escalate the crisis. We identify the interactional
resources used that successfully redirect persons in crisis in
emotional distress to more practical concerns. We begin by

DOI: 10.4324/9780429354892-4

illustrating what we know about expressions of emotion, such as distress, displays of urgency, and desperation, then show examples of how professionals manage emotion during a crisis through question design and voice inflection.

First, we show how training methods such as repetitive persistence work in real-time interaction by showing when negotiators regain control of a call. Then, we explain when such training methods fail and why emotions spiral for a person in crisis, thus potentially derailing a negotiation. Second, we provide methods for regaining cooperation with a person in crisis, thereby de-escalating emotion through voice inflection. Our examples provide actual cases where variations in tone convey concern, or responsiveness to a person in crisis's situation, and how voice works to calm emotion. Finally, we show how the nuances of grammatical features of turn design such as yes/no questions work to enlist a person in crisis to engage with crisis resolution, thereby refocusing attention, which helps in emotion management.

We ask:

What are the best practices for calming an emotional person in crisis in order to gain and sustain their cooperation for the duration of the encounter?

WHY IS THIS TOPIC IMPORTANT?

It is not hard to imagine that a person threatening suicide is experiencing one of the worst days of their life, and not only might they feel upset and emotional, but they have also earned the right to feel that way. The expression of emotion is ubiquitous in any given interaction but is perhaps more pronounced and consequential in emergency calls and negotiations with people in crisis. Crisis professionals are the voice of calm during the encounter. They swiftly gather relevant information to dispatch the appropriate form of help (emergency calls) and turn emotional distress into problem solving and resolution (crisis negotiations). The task is not straightforward, as strong emotions are hard to defuse and might also escalate.

In emergency calls there are often two persons in crisis: the person calling and the victim whom the caller is trying to help. When callers are phoning on behalf of another, we refer to the victim as the person in crisis. When callers are phoning on their own behalf (e.g. suicide) we reference the caller as the person in crisis. A caller's emotional expression communicates information about an unfolding emergency and offers insight into the setting from which call takers can infer additional details about the scene (Hareli & Hess, 2010). However, Svensson and Pesämaa (2018) warn that focusing only on emotional expression and decision making "fails to recognize the nuanced information that discrete emotions (such as anger, fear, and sadness) may provide" (p. 1), thus suggesting that emotions also offer nuanced opportunities for crisis professionals to manage and guide persons in crisis towards a quicker resolution and a smoother interaction towards the provision of help. Moreover, prior training does not fully explain how call takers should manage callers' emotional display to avoid stalling and keep the call or crisis negotiation moving forward.

WHAT CURRENT TRAINING TELLS US ABOUT EMOTION IN EMERGENCIES

In a crisis situation, a person's emotional state can range from calm to hysterical and inconsolable, influencing the interaction. In emergency phone calls, the context representing the primary research behind this chapter, emotions can affect how call takers understand an unfolding emergency (Whalen & Zimmerman, 1998). Studies have found that a call taker's interpretation of a caller's emotion directly and indirectly affects the outcome of the call. For example, fear and sadness will convey help is needed immediately, whereas a caller's expression of anger is treated as less urgent (Svensson & Pesämaa, 2018). As Clawson and Sinclair (2001) contend, for call takers, "it is not just the emotional level of the caller, but also the caller's willingness or ability to cooperate with the call taker that is important" (p. 30).

Although the definition of emotion varies across disciplines, many agree that human emotion involves behavioural and cognitive components (Jones, 2001). The behavioural approach treats emotion as a biological function that helps humans regulate their actions. Such a perspective suggests that emotional expression is not always visible to others. This means, emotions are internal, with a physiological response such as an increased heart rate, but no outward communicative affect. The cognitive component explains the intentionality of "emotions being about something" (Solomon, 2010, p. 12) and is best understood as the appraisal process of some event or situation that triggers an emotional response for the observer.

Interactional studies make observations about when emotions become visible and accountable. In an early study of how call takers managed caller hysteria in 911 emergency calls, Whalen and Zimmerman (1998) described how visible emotions have a focused object; meaning, a person is not just happy or angry for no reason. Instead, they are happy or angry about something in particular. Regarding extreme emotions such as hysteria, they contend that some events trigger emergency callers' emotions, and therefore, callers are "emotionally responsive to their particular situation" (1998, p. 143). They go on to explain that while callers are, and have every right to be emotional, call takers labelling a caller as 'hysterical' cast those callers into a category "of a kind of situational incompetence – namely, the inability to cooperate appropriately in the work of the call" (1998, p. 144). Losing a caller's attention or cooperation stalls the call taker's ability to provide help and might halt the call entirely if the caller cannot gain composure to answer questions and carry out instructions if they hang up. Whalen & Zimmerman (1998) found that methods for getting a caller's attention include directives such as "calm down; stop shouting; answer my questions" (p. 153). When call takers manage to realign the caller to answer relevantly, in turn, they are taking control of the call so that callers can help complete tasks related to pre-arrival instructions (Clawson, Dernocoeur, & Murray, 2015; Whalen and Zimmerman, 1998).

An emergency call taker's primary job is to get pertinent information about an incident, including the location and the nature of the emergency, and promptly send the appropriate form of help. However, challenges emerge when callers become too emotional and anxious to focus on a call taker's questions. Previous work outlines ways to understand how people in crisis express emotion. For example, categorizing a caller as 'hysterical' offers a description of callers who hit their emotional threshold and fall into a state of excitement where they lose control over their emotions and behavior (Clawson et al., 2015). In practice, callers' emotions are rated through an emotional content and cooperation score to describe callers' demeanor during a call, which helps quality control auditors assess call quality. The emotional content score uses a scale of 1–5, where 1 denotes a calm and conversational caller and 5 represents callers who are too emotionally distraught to communicate clearly (Eisenberg et al., 1986). A study that measured the emotional content and cooperation scores of 6000 callers to emergency call centres, found the average score for emergency medical calls was 1.21 or below (Clawson & Sinclair, 2001). These findings show that callers can remain conversational and cooperative for the duration of the call, through many call types. However, Clawson et al. (2015) caution that while a low percentage of callers rank 4–5 on the scale, call takers must remain alert and treat each caller as needing help to stay on the right side of the hysteria threshold.

We offer another viewpoint by examining interactional challenges when speaking with and providing help to an emotional person in crisis. Previous work has shown that callers' emotions are a barrier when sending help or giving pre-arrival instructions (Whalen & Zimmerman, 1998; Svennevig, 2012). Another research line raises the problem of how call takers (successfully or unsuccessfully) manage their emotions when dealing with others' emotions (Hedman, 2016; Tracy & Tracy, 1998; Whalen & Zimmerman, 1998; Whalen, Zimmerman, & Whalen, 1988). A person in crisis's emotions during a crisis pose a number of challenges. For example, a person in crisis can get overtly angry at a crisis professional's questions, perhaps because they do not know the answer or they feel it delays the provision of help (Tracy, 2002). Another challenge includes domestic violence cases when callers become paralysed with fear, rendering them unable to respond to crisis professionals. In every scenario where a caller's emotional outburst derails the caller taker's agenda, call takers need to remain composed and focus on the goal of gaining the caller's cooperation in the service of providing help.

WHAT REPETITIVE PERSISTENCE LOOKS LIKE IN EMERGENCY CALLS

The most common method for managing callers' emotions taught in 9-1-1 (US emergency call) emergency medical dispatch training is directives (e.g., instructing callers to calm down) termed '*repetitive persistence*' designed to gain the cooperation of hysterical callers. 'Repetitive persistence' emerged from a 1974 study of emergency medical calls that examined how call takers help hysterical callers regain control and cooperate with instructions (Clawson et al., 2015). The observation found that when call takers repeated unanswered questions in the same tone, they would eventually respond. Repetitive persistence is now an umbrella term describing three different methods for regaining a caller's attention and cooperation including: 1) repeating the same question in the same tone until the caller responds; 2) soliciting the caller's attention by name, "Ma'am Ma'am M'am"; 3) instructing the caller to calm down and offer a reason, "Calm down so you can help your friend." Examples 4.1–4.3 demonstrate if and how this method works in practice. In the examples below, we refer to call takers as "dispatchers" (DIS), and when the caller is phoning on behalf of another, we refer to the caller as the "caller" (CLR) and the victim as the person in crisis (PiC). When the caller calls on behalf of themselves, we refer to them as the person in crisis (PiC).

Example 4.1 shows how a caller becomes emotionally distraught when describing how her friend appears to be overdosing on drugs. The example begins by showing how CLR goes from clearly responding to DIS's request for the location, but then becomes audibly upset when she explains the unfolding scene (lines 09–11).

```
Example 4.1: He's making noises
01   DIS:    P'lice recorded emergency line.
02           Whe[re is your emergency.
03   CLR:       [Hi:: Hi Hi- This is Melissa Wan.
04           >In< two: hundred
05           Kane Street Eastbridge ((State))
06   DIS:    Two hundred Kane Street.
```

```
07              Eastbridge ((State)).=What's
08              goin' on¿
09    CLR:      Uh:m an' so eh:=HHH.hh my friend
10              is O- he O'dee:d I don't know what's
11              going on.=[HHHH.HHHH HHHHH
```

Callers' emotions can interfere with a call taker's ability to
hear and understand the report. As the call continues, DIS
attempts to regain CLR's attention by using a form of repetitive
persistence, "calm down + reason", when he says: "I need you to
get yourself together to help your friend. Calm yourself okay?"
(lines 13–15).

```
Example 4.1: He's making noises (cont'd)
09    CLR:   Uh:m an' so eh:=HHH.hh my friend
10           is O- he O'dee:d I don't know what's
11           going on.=[HHHH.HHHH HHHHH
12    DIS:            [Okay is there an ap-
13           Listen. I need you to get yourself
14           t'gether t'help yer fri:end.=
15           Calm yourself oka[:y?]
16    CLR:                    [Oka]y. Wha-
17           whaddo I do ~I [need help~.HHH HHHH]
18    DIS:                  [Okay. Jus jus jus ju]st
19           take a deep breath and answer my questions
20           okay that's [all I] need you to do.=
21    CLR:              [EHHH ]
22    DIS:   =Wh- Is there an apartment or floor?
```

Initially the method works. CLR tries to regain her composure
when she asks, "Okay. Wha- whaddo I do ~I need help~" (lines
16–17). DIS, focusing on CLR's emotional state, instructs her
to "just take a deep breath and answer my questions" (lines
18–19). After working to get her calm enough to respond to
questions, DIS restarts the question he abandoned earlier (line

12) and changes his focus to getting the exact location so he can dispatch help, "Is there an apartment or floor?" (line 22).

In practice, repetitive persistence is the primary practice for regaining a caller's attention. However, the success realized through this method is often short-lived as that attention is rarely sustained. In this example, DIS assumes that he has CLR's full attention when he asks for the apartment or floor of her location (line 22). When he asks his question, we can hear background noise of a person struggling to breathe. In a place where CLR should respond, she focuses on the patient (lines 25–26), thereby stalling the progression of the call. DIS then reasserts his question, "Okay is there an apartment or floo:r?" (lines 27–28), to which CLR replies, "it's an apartment." (line 30).

```
Example 4.1: He's making noises (cont'd)
22  DIS:    =Wh- Is there an apartment or floor?
23              (.)
24              ((breathing sound in background))
25  CLR:    .hhh (0.2) Wait listen he's
26          ma:king noi:s[es.
27  DIS:                  [Okay is there
28          an apartment or floo:r.
29              (0.5)
30  CLR:    Ih- it- it's an apartment.
31  DIS:    .hh What is it?
```

In another instance, we see how DIS attempts multiple rounds of repetitive persistence to regain and secure CLR's cooperation. In Example 4.2, CLR phones because her father is overdosing on heroin and she is distraught.

```
Example 4.2: Dad OD'ing on the floor
01  DIS:    [Nine o]ne one this line is recorded.
02  CLR:    [DA: D.]
03  DIS:    [Where is your emergency.]
```

```
04   CLR:   [Oh my God=hh. I think my=kh ]
05   CLR:   I th<u>i</u>nk my d<u>a</u>:d's OD-ing on th' floor.
06          .hh He's not responding.=hh.hh
07          I'm at f<u>o</u>rty one >Gopher Street<.
08          Would you please hurry I >don't wan'
09          [ h<u>im</u> t'die.< hhh
10   DIS:   [Ma'am. <u>MA</u>'AM. You need. [to cal:m down.]
11   CLR:                                 [HHH.HH HHH    ]
```

When DIS asks for her location, we can hear CLR cry out, "Oh my God I think my dad is od'ing on the floor." (lines 04–05). Although crying, she gives her address (lines 06–07), then pleads to send help quick (lines 08–09). CLR becomes audibly emotional (line 08). To regain her attention and get her cooperation, DIS employs a form of repetitive persistence by soliciting her attention, "Ma'am. MA'AM. You need to cal:m down."(line 10).

Similar to Example 4.1, CLR's emotional display renders her speechless as she starts crying. To manage the interaction, DIS attempts another training calming technique, repeating questions in the same tone until CLR responds (lines 12 and 15). CLR responds with a specific location at line 16, and then shifts focus on her father and his unfolding condition.

```
Example 4.2: Dad OD'ing on the floor (cont'd)
12   DIS:   Wha:t's thee ad[dress.
13   CLR:                  [OH MY GOD
14          My dad's on th'] mm-
15   DIS:   Wha:t [is the ad:dress.
16   CLR:         [↑Forty one↓ Go:pher Street.
```

Example 4.3 comes from a case where a neighbour (CLR) phones because she fears that her neighbour (PiC) is suicidal. In the example below, we see what happens when DIS struggles to keep the caller focused on the central task related to getting help. As with the previous examples, the caller in Example 4.3 is distracted by PiC, and we hear her talk directed elsewhere. The interactional problem is a matter of how DIS regains control of the call.

```
Example 4.3: Suicidal Neighbour
01  CLR:   Um: She needs help. She needs it-
02         rea::lly needs t'be put in detox.
03         She's in terrible sha:pe. .hh She's
04         sha:kin' she's cr:ying she wants
05         to commit suicide she wants [t'~die~.
06  DIS:                               [Uhkay.
07  CLR:   And I've never- PIC,
08         I ha:ve to tell 'em th' truth.
09  PIC:   No?
10  CLR:   Ye:s.
11  DIS:   Kay. Ma'am¿
12  CLR:   I have to.
13  PIC:   (          )
14  CLR:   And uhm-
15  PIC:   Fuck. No?
16  CLR:   All right. [PIC,  ]please.
17  DIS:              [Ma'am.]
```

DIS listens to CLR's report about the unfolding trouble but has trouble getting his line of questioning started for the purpose of dispatching help. At line 06, DIS's "Okay" indicates receipt of the information and marks a transition to something new (Beach, 1993) such as asking a location question. However, CLR continues her report (line 07), and DIS withholds pursuing his institutional work. Training advises dispatchers to regain control of the call by using a caller's name (if they know their name) or the pronoun "Ma'am", as in lines 11 and 17. But we see his attempt fail as CLR continues to speak to PiC.

```
Example 4.3: Suicidal Neighbour (cont'd)
18  CLR:    And I- I've ta:lked to her son
19           Edwa:rd at wo:rk,
20  DIS:    Yeah.
21  CLR:    He- he's wanting you d'help her
22           I don't want[chu d]'go out.
23  DIS:                 [Okay.] Okay. Ma'am.
24  CLR:    Ye:s=And I can give you Ed:ward's
25           number at [wor ]k.
26  DIS:               [No. ]Ma'am. Ma'am.
27  CLR:    Yes.
28  DIS:    Okay. Are you in her apartment?
29  CLR:    Yes I am. Oh it's ~ba:d.~
30  DIS:    Okay. Ma'am. Is she being violent
31           or anything er:
32  CLR:    Stop it. Stop it, PIC.
33  PIC:    I can't. I can't.
```

DIS continues to use various forms of repetitive persistence to regain the caller's attention. At line 17, he solicits her attention with, "Ma'am". At line 23, he tries to stop her from the narrative she launched with, "Okay. Okay. Ma'am.", which fails as the caller goes on to offer the telephone number of PiC's son. In the next turn, DIS attempts to regain control of the call. First, he rejects her offer for the phone number and then redirects her attention to him, "No. Ma'am. Ma'am." (line 26), to which CLR responds with, "Yes." (line 27). DIS treats her response as now having her attention, and then asks if CLR is in PiC's apartment (line 28). CLR responds to his question in the next turn (line 29). It appears, at this point, that DIS has CLR's attention and cooperation. However, her cooperation is short term. After asking CLR if PiC is violent (line 30), she yells at PiC to "Stop it." (line 32) and is no longer paying attention to DIS. The gaining and losing a caller's attention is a common barrier in advancing these calls.

Cases like Example 4.3 demonstrate the problem of fleeting attention that dispatchers need to manage during high stress and emotional calls. While dispatchers focus on their task of getting pertinent information, callers respond to immediate unfolding events before them, succumbing to the emotional strain of stress, quickly losing their ability to respond to questions. We see this struggle play out as DIS continues to regain CLR's focus.

```
Example 4.3: Suicidal Neighbour (cont'd)
34  DIS:    Ma'am.
35  CLR:    Yes:.
36  DIS:    Okay. Please talk t'me,>is she
37          being violent or anything er:
38  CLR:    No: but she's a danger to herself
39          and there's no question about it.
40          (PIC name) (PIC name)
41  DIS:    Okay. Ma'am.
42  CLR:    Yea:s.
43  DIS:    Okay. I can hear [her- Is she] giving-
44  CLR:                     [The Police.]
45  DIS:    Ma'am.
46  PIC:    I don't want (        )
47  DIS:    Ma'am.
48  CLR:    What? Yeah.
49  DIS:    Okay. Is she giving you a hard time?
50          Because I can hear her. I don't- (.) want
51          you t'be put in da:nger.
52  CLR:    No.
```

As CLR focuses on PiC, DIS works to regain her attention when he says, "Ma'am." (line 34). CLR immediately responds with, "Yes:." (line 35), and similar to a few lines above, DIS might assume he has her attention. In a place where he could move forward with a next question, he once again must confirm he has her attention, "Okay. Please, talk to me." (line 36). He then continues with same question as before, asking if PiC is violent. As this call progresses, we see DIS struggle to sustain CLR's cooperation over a series of questions and answers. Rather than moving towards sending help, it is a constant push and pull as DIS struggles to keep CLR's focus on the primary task.

LESSONS LEARNED FROM EXAMPLES 4.1–4.3

- A challenge for emergency call takers is sustaining a caller's attention for the duration of the encounter
- An emergency caller's dual focus of attention is a barrier for productive communication
- Training techniques such as repetitive persistence have initial success getting a caller's attention early in the call, but that success wanes as call takers work to get pertinent case information.

VOICE FEATURES OF REMAINING CALM IN CRISIS NEGOTIATIONS

We now turn our attention to crisis negotiations, particularly in cases where negotiators summon a person in crisis to maintain their attention when their situation is getting increasingly critical. One of the first lessons in emergency caller training is that you are the voice of authority and should remain calm and professional for the duration of the call (Clawson et al., 2015). In crisis negotiation training, a key point for negotiators includes that they remain calm by controlling their emotions, and their voice pitch and quality (McMains & Mullins, 2014). However, there is little research on the phonetic, linguistic, and interactional features of 'remaining calm'.

Elsewhere, we have shown how negotiators manage variation in voice pitch when seeking attention from the person in crisis who are unwilling, unable, or unavailable to answer (Sikveland, 2019). This research shows how negotiators manage the fine line between remaining calm and persistent, and responding to an escalation of the crisis situation. Indeed, secondary negotiators (see also Chapter 7) monitor the same features when telling the primary negotiator to remain calm.

Example 4.4 demonstrates the relevance of voice management. PiC, here anonymized as Jessica, is barricaded inside her flat with a noose around her neck and holding a knife. In this case, PiC and N1 already have mutual and visual contact as N1 can see PiC through a gated but locked door into her flat. N1's main project is to get PiC to hand him the keys through the gate. In the last couple of minutes prior to Example 4.4, PiC has tightened the noose around her neck, and N1 has suggested she undo/ loosen it. PiC sounds as if she has trouble breathing (transcribed using a '*'). In response to growing concern and urgency, the negotiator increasingly escalates with repetitive persistence by summoning her by name.

```
Example 4.4: Throw me the keys
01   N1:      =>Jessica< throw me the keys.
02   PiC:     *.hhhh*
03                    (.)
04   N1:      Come on darling throw me the keys.
05                    (0.2)
06   N1:      Please.
07                    (2.9)
08   PiC:     *.hhhhhhh*
09                    (1.2)
10   PiC:     (how/no)
11                    (0.4)
12   N1:      Jessic[a,
13   PiC:           [*.hhh
14                    (0.6)
15   N1:      ↑Jessica,
16                    (0.2)
17   N1:      ↑Jessica:?=
18   PiC:     =*.hhhhh*=
19   N1:      =You need to stay awake now?
```

N1 has moved from requesting the keys to an imperatively formed directive in line 01, "throw me the keys.", which he repeats in line 04. In lines 02 and 08, PiC does not provide any answer, but produces a series of strained inbreaths, which is also observed in lines 13 and 18. Line 10 represents a potential lexical response to N1's request. It is produced on a breathy, nasalized voice and its indistinct production makes both "no" and "how" possible hearings. N1 then seeks to secure attention to a current interactional focus with the summonses in lines 12, 15, and 17. While these summonses open for new opportunities for PiC to respond to N1's request, they seem to intensify N1's efforts and project a shift from pursuing a request to N1 displaying concern about PiC's basic abilities to stay engaged and breathing. This shift is evidenced through N1 urging PiC to stay awake ("you need to stay awake now?", line 19), indicating a critical, dangerous moment is emerging. The increasing orientation to danger is associated with some intensification in the subsequent summonses: Line 15 has a slightly higher pitch than line 12 (indicated with ↑), and line 17 has a higher pitch than line 15 with a marked increase at the end of the summons (indicated with '?'). Lines 15 and 17 are both also noticeably louder than line 12.

While N1 seems to gradually escalate the seriousness of the situation in Example 4.4, a significantly more marked contrast occurs approximately four minutes later in this encounter. This case gives further support that participants monitor the level of phonetic upgrading in self-repeated summons. In this case, a self-repeated summons warrants an intervention from the second negotiator, to "keep calm". This excerpt also involves PiC's dog (D), who the negotiators have brought into the scene from the outside.

```
Example 4.4: Throw me the keys (cont'd)
223 N1:    Throw the keys.
224            (1.9) / ((N: *.hhhh)) / ((D: snarling))
225 N1:    TH:ROW the keys.
226            (0.2)
```

```
227  PiC:    *.HHHHH*
228  N1:     Jessi[ca¿          ]
229  D:           [((barking))]  ((barking))
230                  (0.4)
231  N1:     JESSICA.
232                  (0.2)
233  D:      ((barking))
234                  (0.4)
235  N2:     °°keep calm°°
236  N1:     Jessica.
237                  (0.3)
238  N1:     Throw the keys.
```

While N1 has persisted with the directive 'Throw the keys' (lines 223 and 225: noticeably louder in the latter production), PiC's trouble of breathing gets worse (line 227). N1 repeats his summons in line 231, this time with a significantly louder and higher pitch than in line 228, and it is also much louder with more vocal effort. The secondary negotiator, N2, orients to this change and addresses N1 with "°°keep calm°°" (line 235). In other words, the phonetic contrast is not just measurable as larger than normal, it is also treated as such by the co-participants. The final summons, line 236, shows similar pitch features to 231, but noticeably quieter: N1 does not escalate the summoning any further.

LESSONS LEARNED FROM EXAMPLE 4.4

- Negotiators use phonetic features of their voice systematically to maintain attention of the person in crisis
- Changing voice features can escalate the situation beyond persistence, orienting to the critical nature of the crisis
- The phonetic design of summonses is treated by the negotiators themselves as relevant in displaying concern, or responsiveness to an emerging crisis.

In the next section we describe question design strategies for swift responses and getting callers to move into action.

HOW THE GRAMMAR OF A TURN CAN CHANGE THE OUTCOME OF AN EMERGENCY CALL

In critical calls, emergency call takers need more than a caller's attention. They need to sustain their attention and enlist them as a cooperative partner. As first-hand witnesses at a scene, emergency callers are their eyes and ears for crisis professionals. In emergency medical calls callers carry out life-saving instructions. The skillful coordination is dependent upon the seamlessness of communication between the two parties for the duration of the call. As we look into the nuances of how these calls unfold, we see how not only word choice (see Chapter 3), but also the grammar of a turn are resources that crisis professionals use to increase their chance of having successful outcomes.

1. Yes/no questions that target a person in crisis's knowledge or ability to gather information

In a time-sensitive environment, emergency dispatchers need specific and immediate information from callers. Scripted guide cards are tailored for efficiency by using the yes/no format for question design. For example, in emergency medical calls dispatchers ask a series of questions that help narrow down the patient's condition for the correct protocol. Two of the most important questions involve finding out the status of the patient's consciousness and breathing. These questions are designed for yes/no type answers: Is the patient awake (conscious)? Is the patient breathing?

Examples 4.5 and 4.6 demonstrate the efficiency of the question design and how fast callers respond when they are certain of the patient's condition:

```
Example 4.5: Scared to Death
01   DIS:     Is th' person still brea:thing.
02   CLR:     NO:HH.
03   DIS:     Lemme connect us t' Chester.
04            Stay on th' phone.
05   CLR:     ↑HURRY UP:↓ AHHH::
```

```
Example 4.6: I need to give her CPR
01   DIS:    Sir, is she awake?
02   CLR:    Yes. Huh?
03   DIS:    Is she awake?
04   CLR:    No. No. She's not breathing.
05   DIS:    Okay. Is there a defibrillator available?
06   CLR:    Uh, no, there isn't.
```

Questions such as these generally pose little trouble for callers to answer. However, when callers are emotional and unsure about the status of a patient, callers might respond with ambiguous answers such as "I don't know", thereby leaving it up to the dispatcher to figure out how to unpack those answers for a more accurate response. Thus, yes/no formatted questions pose problems for dispatchers who are panicking and uncertain about how to answer the call taker's question correctly.

Examples 4.7–4.9 are cases where callers start with a yes or no response, but then modify their response, showing their uncertainty about the situation.

```
Example 4.7: I think she overdosed
01   DIS:    What do you think she overdosed on?
02   CLR:    Heroin.
03   DIS:    Okay. Is she breathing?
04   CLR:    No. It's like barely.
```

In Example 4.7, CLR responds to the "Is she breathing?" (line 03) question with a quick "No" (line 04), but then immediately alters her response to show that it's not a definitive "No" because there is some breath, "It's like barely."

In Example 4.8, CLR responds to DIS's second attempt asking the breathing question responding with a quick "Yeah." (line 05) But then DIS continues with a downgrade from the firm "yes" to "a little bit" (line 05), then the patient is "starting to come around now." Finally, the caller shows uncertainty, "I don't know."

```
Example 4.8: Son Overdosed
01   DIS:    Is he brea:thing?
02   CLR:    He jus' had a needle in his leg, I think.
03   DIS:    Is he brea:thing?
04   CLR:    (Patient), are you breathin'.
05           Yea:h. Yea a little bit. Yeah.
06           He's starting to come around now.
07           I don't know.
08               (0.8)
09   DIS:    .hh Okay. I want you to check him okay.
10   CLR:    He's starting-
11   DIS:    Check him, okay? (.) I want you to say
12           no:w every single time he takes a
13           breath in starting immediately.
```

Even in cases where callers know the exact medical problem, they may struggle with the yes/no formatted questions. In Example 4.10, DIS knows the person in crisis just snorted an unknown substance and has passed out as a result. In response to the first question, "Is he awake?" CLR responds with a definitive "No". When asked if the person is breathing, CLR describes PiC's color, "He's blue" and then admits, "I cannot tell."

```
Example 4.9: Snorted Something _ Giving CPR
01   DIS:    Okay. Is he awa:ke.
02   CLR:    No:h.
03   DIS:    Is he brea:thing.
04   CLR:    He's blue. I ca:n (.) not tell.
```

In Example 4.10, CLR delays his response and shows uncertainty when he responds, "he might be." In the same turn, CLR downgrades his response from something that leans towards a possible yes, to towards a possible no with, "I don't think so.

I think he's gone for now." (lines 03–04). Notice that the last component allows for an inference that PiC is possibly deceased.

```
Example 4.10: Think it's an overdose
01   DIS:    Is she breathin'¿
02   CLR:    Uh: he's eh:hh he mi:ght be:,
03           I don't think so:.
04           I think he's gone fe:r now.
```

In each case, dispatchers use a yes/no designed question to get the necessary information in a quick and efficient manner. When callers are able to answer these questions in an unproblematic manner, dispatchers keep the call moving forward. However, as we have shown in the above examples, even though callers have first-hand access to PiC, they might resist answering these questions in a definitive manner.

When callers are uncertain, or become emotional because of the unfolding circumstances, crisis professionals need to shift gears and find new ways to engage callers so they cooperate in for the duration of the call. We suggest thinking about talk as action. By getting callers involved in a task related to patient/person in crisis care, callers are willing to become involved as it helps them focus on a specific goal tied to getting help.

2. Yes/no questions as directives that give callers a task for patient care

A challenge for dispatchers is managing callers' emotional distress while simultaneously working to get information to send help or give life-saving instructions over the phone. When callers make emotional pleas for dispatchers to send help immediately, they lose focus on the questions and instructions designed exactly for that purpose. In this section we show how redesigning a yes/no type question to a directive format (e.g. "can you tell me...") helps dispatchers manage callers' emotional pleas and gets them to focus on specific actions to help the person in crisis.

Dispatchers have to get callers close enough to patients/persons in crisis so they can do a diagnostic assessment of the person's condition. In Example 4.11, CLR phoned to report that she found her sister passed out in the bathroom from a possible drug overdose. CLR is upset and crying, and thus far, DIS uses repetitive persistence to calm CLR so she can answer questions. In this example, DIS uses directives to redirect her attention and gain her cooperation.

```
Example 4.11: Found my sister in the bathroom
01 DIS:     Okay. What's wrong with your sister.
02 CLR:     She's passed out on th' bathroom
03          floor I jus' heard a big ba:ng I came
04          in it's- she's got a ~needle stick-~
05 DIS:     How old is she:.
06 CLR:     HH Uh she's twenny-[twenny four?]
07 DIS:                       [Can you tell]
08          me if she's breathing?
09 CLR:     I DON'T KNO:W?
10 DIS:     Okay=Can you fee:l her? Is she-
11          Is she blue is she white is she pale?
12 CLR:     MARY? She's turnin' pa:le.
13 DIS:     Okay. I'm gunna get th' ambulance on the phone.
```

In response to the question, "Can you tell me if she's breathing?" (lines 07–08) CLR immediately screams out, "I don't know" (line 09). CLR's increased volume conveys a sense of hysteria and urgency but stalls the progression of the call as her response does not give the call taker a clear path on how to proceed. DIS works to get a better response by redesigning the question to a directive, giving CLR a specific task, "Can you feel her? Is she blue is she white is she pale?" (lines 10–11). By asking CLR to check on PiC's coloring, DIS gives her a task to inspect PiC by look or feel and to report back. PiC's colouring will, in turn, inform DIS about the breathing. We see in the next turn the strategy works as CLR responds immediately, "she's turnin' pa:le" (line 12) which is a sign PiC is still breathing.

In Example 4.12 DIS uses a directive to enlist CLR's help with the diagnostic component. Here CLR phones about her friend who is overdosing on drugs.

```
Example 4.12: Oh My God He's Dead
01   CLR:   ↑ETHAN↓.hh Oh MY GOD he's ~Dead=hh~
02   DIS:   Ma'am.
03   CLR:   Oh my Go:[d=hh
04   DIS:            [Is there- Can you che:ck
05              to see t'see if there's
06              a pulse or any brea:thing?
07                  (1.5)
08   CLR:   Uh:m
09                 (2.1)
10   DIS:   Can yih put [yer h]a:nd under like
11   CLR:               [Ye:ah.]
12   DIS:   his nose an' see if there's any breathing.
13                 (0.2)
14   CLR:   I don't kno:w. (.) ↑YES↓ he's breathing.
15   DIS:   O:kay.
16   CLR:   He's breathing.
17   DIS:   Okay. An' n'how old is he?
18   CLR:   TWEnny seven.
```

We can hear CLR screaming to her friend and crying (line 01), clearly distraught over finding her friend in this condition. DIS begins to design a yes/no type question, possibly asking if the person is breathing, when he starts to say, "Is there-" (line 04). But DIS stops himself and changes the course of action to get CLR involved. DIS uses the "can you" design to initiate a task for CLR, "Can you check to see t'see if there's a pulse or any breathing?" (lines 04–06). In tense moments such as these, one might expect CLR to unravel, become more emotional, and resist. However, in many cases callers plead for dispatchers to tell them what they should do, and when they give callers a task to carry out, callers are willing to comply. Although there is a delay of 1.5 seconds at line 07, CLR says, "Uh:m" at line 08, holding her turn, presumably carrying out the task. After another 2.1 seconds of silence (line 09) DIS prompts CLR by giving her further instructions on how to check for breathing, "can you put yer hand under like his nose and see if there's any breathing" (lines 10/12). Initially, CLR says she does not know, but then exclaims, "↑YES↓ he's breathing." (line 14), which is a sign of life, and of hope, and CLR makes a noticeable shift from emotionally upset to calm. She is cooperative for the remainder of the call.

Another challenge when speaking with an emotional caller is getting additional information about the unfolding situation. In scripted protocols, the question, 'tell me exactly what happened' is meant to solicit a narrative that contextualizes the emergency. In Chapter 2 we saw how requests for a person in crisis to 'tell' 'what happened' can work as an effective way into the conversation. However, in emergency phone calls callers are sometimes not able to provide a description. In Example 4.13, in response to DIS's question, "Tell me exactly what happened." (line 01), CLR starts a narrative by explaining what happened at the start of the day, "I woke up he's been" (line 02), but then stops and pleads for help. Although CLR continues, she struggles to explain that she is unsure if her husband is having a stroke (line 07).

```
Example 4.13: Husband having a stroke
01   DIS:    Okay. Tell me exactly what happened.
02   CLR:    I woke up he's been (0.5) PLE(hh)SE ~Hurry~
03   DIS:    [Al-   ]
04   CLR:    [.hh He]'s ti- I'm (spying) it's-
05           it's- it's- not a s- i(h)t's-.hh
06           he's had a heart b'f-
07           [I th]ink he's having a stro:ke
```

```
08   DIS:    [Okay.]
09   CLR:    or [a fit. ] I don't know what [he is.
10   DIS:       [Tell me]                    [Tell me
11   DIS:    what you're seeing right now. Tell
12           me what ha:ppened I need to k[no ]w
13   CLR:                                 [He-]
14   DIS:    so I can help you.
15   CLR:    His body was sha:king all over,
16           he's not conscious he can't respond
17           t'me..hh He's jus'-(.) making
18           stra:nge sounds outta his throa:t he's
19   DIS:    O:kay.
20   CLR:    He:'s=hhhh He's not conscious [.hh ]=
21   DIS:                                  [Okay.]
22   CLR:    I think he's DY:ing.=hh
```

To help the caller explain her husband's condition so she understands the situation, DIS uses a different strategy than what we saw in Extract 4.12. DIS begins what sounds like a repeat of her question, but rather than asking about what happened, she changes the turn design, "Tell me what you're seeing right now." (lines 10–11). In changing the turn design, she changes the course of action for the caller's response. By asking CLR to report what she's seeing, DIS narrows the range of possible responses to have CLR explain what she can see, which clarifies what counts as relevant.

The effectiveness of refocusing on what can be done is something we see in crisis negotiations as well as in emergency calls. In emergency calls, dispatchers give a task to the caller. In suicide negotiations, the negotiator can change the course of a person in crisis's actions through offers and invitations. Example 4.14 shows a rare case of affiliation from a suicidal person in crisis: PiC explicitly accepts the negotiator's offer of support. PiC is here barricaded inside his flat, communicating with the negotiator by telephone.

Example 4.14: You must have been so frightened
01 PiC: ~.NHhhhh have you any idea.~
02   (.)
03 PiC: ~(Ey) () you ain't- you ain't
04   got a clue have ya.~
05   (0.3)
06 PiC: ~.Hh[h you] know?~
07 N: [.hh-]
08   (0.2)
09 N: [Simon] I can hear it in your
10 PiC: [~.MHHH~]
11 N: voice how: [how dis]tressed that made you.=
12   [~.MHHH~]
13 N: How upset: (0.2) angry.=You- you- you m-
14   you must have been so frightened.
15   (0.3)
16 PiC: ~.MHHHH~
17   (0.2)
18 N: [You must have been] so frightened.
19 PiC: [~HHhhhh~   ]
20   (0.4)
21 PiC: ~You have no idea miss seriously.~
22   (0.8)
23 N: That's why I wanna t- I wanna- I wanna
24   come and sort this out.=I wanna
25   [talk to] you about it.=And I've- promise you.
26 PiC: [~.MHHH~]
27 N: .hhhh it's me::? (.) coming to talk >to you<.=
28   That's why I've given you this pri:vate
29   pho:ne, (.) so it's you and me.
30   (0.5) and we can get this sorted out.

```
31                    (2.1)
32   PiC:   Okay.
33   N:     [Is that] alri[:ght.]
34   PiC:   [(yes-) ]        [Yes ] that'd be nice.
```

One key feature in this example is PiC's expression of upset/
trembling voice, represented by the '~' symbol observed in most
of PiC's turns. In lines 01–05 PiC presents his suicidal behaviour
in the past as inaccessible to the negotiator/others ("you ain't
got a clue", line 03). In response, the negotiator affiliates with
PiC's emotions, "I can hear it in your voice how distressed
that made you." (lines 09/11). The negotiator thereby focusses
on hearable features in PiC's voice, and how she can relate to
those, not claiming she understands PiC's situation. In this case,
PiC's emotions are accessible and relevant for N to label. The
negotiator pursues her emotional affiliation in line 18, before PiC
reissues his stance "~You have no idea miss seriously.~" (line
21). But N does not stop there; she follows up on her emotional
affiliation by targeting something she can do: "That's why I [...]
come and sort this out." (lines 23–24). N proceeds reassuring PiC
it is only her who is coming, "so it's you and me. (0.5) and we can
get this sorted out." (lines 29–30) (dealing with PiC's previously
stated concern with letting the police inside the flat). N pursues
this proposal in line 33 ("Is that alrigh:t."), before PiC explicitly
agrees "Yes that'd be nice." (line 34). In line with our findings
reported in Chapter 3, we see how the negotiator successfully
here uses the formulation "*sort*", not "*help*", when offering
support. The negotiator refocuses emotional labelling/affiliation
into actions that can be done, and that is key to progressing the
crisis encounter.

SUMMARY

A psychological perspective suggests that, during a stressful
situation, emotions can drive a person's behavior away from
rational thought as they pull away from a feeling of having
control. In this chapter, we have shown how training techniques
like 'repetitive persistence' have, in practice, varying outcomes
for regaining control of the call and calming emotional persons
in crisis. De-escalation training and negotiation methods,

> **TAKEAWAY PRACTICAL STRATEGIES: MANAGING EMOTIONS**
>
> - Techniques such as 'repetitive persistence' and 'soliciting attention' are temporary solutions that do not advance the long-term goal of an emergency call
> - Voice features can display increased concern, and negotiators use the voice actively to adjust their response to the crisis
> - Dispatchers regain control of a distracted caller by giving them a specific task
> - The way dispatchers give instructing information helps sustain a caller's attention for the duration of the interaction

such as 'open-ended questions' and 'active listening' do not always help advance the negotiation for a positive outcome. Our research points to additional resources crisis professionals use that engage a person in crisis by gaining their cooperation and getting them involved in tasks. Such methods work to manage emotions by diffusing the focus on how they feel 'about' the situation to giving them something that helps them 'control' the situation through action.

REFERENCES

Beach, W. A. (1993). Transitional regularities for casual "Okay" usages. *Journal of Pragmatics, 19*, 325–352.

Clawson, J. J., Dernocoeur, K.B., & Murray, C. (2015). *Principles of Emergency Medical Dispatch 6th edition*. Priority Press.

Clawson, J. J., & Sinclair, R. (2001). The emotional content and cooperation score in emergency Medical dispatching. *Prehospital Emergency Care, 5*(1), 29–35.

Eisenberg, M. S., Carter, W., Hallstrom, A., Cummins, R., Litwin, P., & Hearne, T. (1986). Identification of cardiac arrest by emergency dispatchers. *The American journal of emergency medicine, 4*(4), 299–301.

Hareli, S., & Hess, U. (2010). What emotional reactions can tell us about the nature of others: An appraisal perspective on person perception. *Cognition and Emotion, 24*(1), 128–140.

Hedman, K. (2016). Managing emotions in Swedish medical emergency calls. *IMPACT Journal, 2*, 1–12.

Jones, T. S., & Bodtker, A. (2001). Mediating with heart in mind: Addressing emotion in mediation practice. *Negotiation Journal, 17*(3), 217–244.

McMains, M., & Mullins, W. C. (2014). *Crisis negotiations: Managing critical incidents and hostage situations in law enforcement and corrections.* New York: Routledge.

Sikveland, R. O. (2019). Failed summons: Phonetic features of persistence and intensification in crisis negotiation. *Journal of Pragmatics, 150,* 167–179.

Solomon, R. C. (2010). The philosophy of emotions. In Lewis, M., Haviland-Jones, J. M., & Barrett, L. F. (Eds.) *Handbook of emotions,* 3rd edition (pp. 3–16). New York: Guilford.

Svennevig, J. (2012). On being heard in emergency calls. The development of hostility in a fatal emergency call. *Journal of Pragmatics, 44,* 1393–1412.

Svensson, M., & Pesämaa, O. (2018). How does a caller's anger, fear and sadness affect operators' decisions in emergency calls? *International Review of Social Psychology, 31*(1), p. 1–7.

Tracy, S. J. (2002). When questioning turns to face threat: An interactional sensitivity in 911 call-taking. *Western Journal of Communication, 66,* 129–157.

Tracy, K., & Tracy, S. J. (1998). Rudeness at 911: Reconceptualizing face and face attack. *Human Communication Research, 25*(2), 225–251.

Whalen, J., & Zimmerman, D. H. (1998). Observations on the display and management of emotion in naturally occurring activities: The case of "hysteria" in calls to 9-1-1. *Social Psychology Quarterly, 61*(2), 141–159.

Whalen, J., Zimmerman, D. H., & Whalen, M. R. (1988). When words fail. A single case analysis. *Social Problems, 35*(4), 335–362.

Overcoming resistance

Chapter 5

WHAT IS THIS CHAPTER ABOUT?

Negotiation is, by definition, an encounter that lasts more than a few turns. It is simply not the case that, on arriving at a crisis scene, or picking up the phone to an emergency caller, that, in response to a person in crisis expressing their intent to take their own life, they will just say "okay then" if the professional party

DOI: 10.4324/9780429354892-5

asks them not to. At least in our datasets, people in crisis are not irrational: they orient to the consistency of their expressed intentions as much as anyone else might and are reluctant to be persuaded otherwise. Therefore, this chapter focuses on the interactional techniques that crisis negotiators use to overcome resistance and how these techniques create positive turning points in encounters. We will show how negotiators actually use and 'leverage' resistance from the person in crisis as an opportunity to facilitate rather than hinder resolution.

We ask:

What interactional techniques do negotiators use to overcome resistance?

WHY IS THIS TOPIC IMPORTANT?

Crisis negotiators may agree that there is no 'secret word' or formulation to overcome resistance: there is no single 'magic wand' for crisis resolution. However, crisis negotiators also routinely overcome resistance, even when dealing with someone who claims they will *never* comply or succumb to a proposed resolution. We refer to these decisive moments of behavioural change in crisis as 'turning points' (Cooper, 2007), asking the primary question: How do such turnings points come about? We offer answers to this question based on what we have found to work in negotiators' turns that lay the foundation for progress rather than resistance in a crisis encounter. Beyond turning points and crisis resolution, this chapter shows how negotiators productively get a person in crisis, at least momentarily, to choose safety over harm (see also Sikveland, Kevoe-Feldman & Stokoe, 2020).

WHAT CURRENT TRAINING TELLS US ABOUT DEALING WITH RESISTANCE IN CRISIS TALK

In their comprehensive guide on hostage and crisis negotiation, McMains and Mullins (2014) present the following description of the slow transition from strong to weaker forms of resistance from a person in crisis (Bob):

> Initially, Bob argued with every suggestion the negotiator presented. Whenever that happened, the negotiator would be

quiet, let Bob vent, and then counter Bob's argument. Over the next several hours, Bob's counter arguments got weaker. The negotiator was paying attention to the emotional content of Bob's communications. *At one point*, the negotiator asked Bob to come outside and meet with the negotiator to discuss one of the suggestions. Bob agreed, put down his weapon, walked outside and surrendered. No one was injured at any time during the incident.

(McMains & Mullins, 2014, p. 242, emphasis added)

How did the negotiator get Bob to agree to put down his weapons and talk to him face/to-face? Did this moment simply just happen, or is it tied to something the negotiator did or did not do? The description suggests that the negotiator's patience and attention to the emotional content of Bob's talk plays a role, with subsequent efforts to counter his arguments. According to the case description, Bob's arguments become weaker over time. But whether the change of behaviour is becoming fatigued, or whether it can be explained by the negotiator's actions, or both, is unclear in this scant description. Though these are not straightforward questions to answer, our aim is to get analytic purchase on the kinds of interactional resources negotiators use so they can leverage and build on weakening forms of resistance.

When it comes to the resources that explicate the outcome-oriented approaches to crisis negotiation, for example, and are widely used by negotiators, the 'influence' and 'behavioural change' stages in the Behavioural Influence Stairway Model (Ireland & Vecchi, 2009) is at the top of the list. In the face of resistance, it is argued that "it is better to sidestep resistance than to argue, debate, or persuade" (McMains & Mullins, 2014, p. 148). That is, by behaving in a non-threatening way, negotiators avoid the person in crisis actively defending their position, and increase the probability of behavioural change.

While "non-threatening" actions are widely presented as having positive outcomes for a successful, and calm, negotiation, we have less empirical basis for understanding what such actions look like in the interaction, and indeed if and how they work to secure positive change. We address this by considering how negotiators manage problem-solving in the face of strong (or weakening) resistance. We also explore where crisis professionals draw the boundary between what is too risky, or not, for crisis resolution. Our analysis reveals how posing challenges (in questions or other formats) can lead to positive, rather than negative shifts in a person in crisis's stance towards the negotiation.

The time it takes to move from resistance to resolution in negotiations with individuals in crisis varies but can take several hours. During this time, a negotiator may recognize stronger and weaker forms of resistance that may have different implications for what to do next. In the next section, we examine how to recognize strong and weak forms of resistance and point to the kinds of shifts in a person in crisis's behaviour which give the negotiator an opportunity to further facilitate a resolution. Then we examine what happens in between that shifts a person in crisis from a strong resistance to weak resistance. Finally, we summarize the specific techniques we have identified that work and do not work to overcome resistance.

FROM STRONGER TO WEAKER FORMS OF RESISTANCE, TO RESOLUTION

This section offers examples that characterize stronger and weaker forms of resistance in crisis negotiations, based on the case study of two different negotiations, one (Case 1) taking place on site with trained crisis negotiators, and another (Case 2) handled by an emergency call taker (dispatcher). In both these cases, we show how a person in crisis's resistance shifts gradually from strong to weak throughout the encounter, finally leading to a resolution when the person in crisis moves to safety. In both these cases, we observe how a person in crisis may start off strong, with unconditional rejections of the negotiation, to weaker arguments and finally a decision to move to safety. This process may be similar to the McMains and Mullins (2014) example presented earlier. We show how a person in crisis's observable shifts in behaviour are tied to what negotiators say and do. We follow two single cases to show how these shifts 'ebb and flow' yet are tangible interactional opportunities to influence the person in crisis's behaviour.

Negotiation Case 1: "Off the balcony"

> *Case summary: In this negotiation, the person in crisis (PiC) is standing on a balcony, barricaded outside his flat. The negotiators can see PiC from the neighbour's balcony, and their first order of business is to get PiC to move to safety, i.e., away from the balcony edge, and removing the noose he sometimes puts around his neck. PiC has put a bicycle across the door to his flat, blocking the door. PiC has a history of mental health problems, including various stays at a mental health institution. Previously that day, mental health personnel had arrived to conduct an assessment. The police and negotiators were called as PiC refused to meet with the health professionals and ended up barricading himself on the balcony threatening to jump.*

Within the first 10 minutes of the negotiation we see instances where PiC shows a *strong resistance* to moving inside. In Extract 5.1 PiC makes it clear that there is nothing the negotiators say or do that can change his decision to stay on the balcony.

```
Example 5.1: Off the balcony [10 mins into the
negotiation]
01   PiC:    I'm staying here.
02                (0.7)
03   N1:     That's fine [you can stay there.]
04   PiC:                [I've given you my- ]
05           ONE HUNDRED percent- (.) when it-
06           becomes BLACK in the NIGHT,
07           (0.2) I'll be here.
```

PiC's assertion in line 01, "I'm staying here", follows a series of responses in which PiC presents his unwillingness to come inside. Prior to this example, PiC's strong resistance came when he said, "I'm doing it" (jumping off the balcony), as compared to, "I'm staying here.", which comes later and does not carry an imminent threat of harm. N1 is thus safe to remain neutral with PiC in line 03: "That's fine you can stay there.". However, maintaining his stance of resistance, PiC clearly shows that his position is non-negotiable. In lines 04–07 he shows he is determined to stay barricaded on the balcony indefinitely: "ONE HUNDRED percent–" (line 05), until it is "BLACK in the NIGHT" (line 06). PiC thereby upgrades his resistance by using words with extreme categories ("100%" and "Black in the night"), further intensified with loud speech production (transcribed with capital letters).

But eventually, *weaker forms of resistance* characterise the negotiation.

```
Example 5.2: Off the balcony [2 hr 30 mins into
the negotiation]
01   PiC:   I can't think bro. I can't mo:ve from
02          here.=That's what I'm saying to you.
03               (0.6)
04   PiC:   It's too much.
05               (0.8)
06   PiC:   There's been too much (0.4) communication.
07               (0.6)
08   PiC:   I can't do anything else.
09               (0.3)
10   PiC:   I wanna be off (of) this fucking thing.
11               (9.4)
```

Prior to this extract, N1 requested that PiC stand his bike up and come meet him in the flat. Now, instead of threatening to "do it", or asserting that he is going to stay on the balcony indefinitely regardless of what the negotiators do or say, PiC breaks his resistance towards the negotiation. We see this through his shift from focussing on his unwillingness to move, to an *inability* to move: "I can't move from here." (line 01) and "I can't do anything else." (line 08). PiC accounts for his inability to move by saying: "It's too much" (line 04) and "There's been too much (0.4) communication." (line 06) suggesting that his decision as to whether or not to remain on the balcony is now outside the realms of his control. Finally, PiC's formulation in line 10, "I wanna be off of this fucking thing.", pushes his stance further towards cooperating with the negotiator, though not directly complying with the negotiation. PiC's conduct is now markedly different from the "I'm doing it" and "I'm staying here" at the early stages of the negotiation, and PiC's resistance has shifted from clear-cut rejection to a potential for collaboration and crisis resolution.

Then, towards the end of a three-and-a-half-hour negotiation, the *crisis is resolved*: PiC moves away from harm by leaving his bike and moving into the flat, to the sound of crowds below cheering and the negotiator preparing to receive him.

```
Example 5.3: Off the balcony [3 hr and 30 minutes into the
negotiation]
01  N1:    Good ma:n.
02                (0.6) / ((sounds of bike being
03                put up against railings))
04  N1:    That's it.
05                (0.3)
06  N1:    Stand it up there,
07                (0.7)
08  N1:    Very well done.=Now if you open that door¿
09                (0.6)
10  N1:    Go in,
11                (1.4)
12         ((Crowd cheers))
13  N1:    I wanna go. I wanna go through.
14                (5.5) / ((N1 moves towards PiC's flat))
```

We gather from this exchange that PiC is moving towards safety. N1's "Good ma:n" (line 01) orients to PiC removing his bike as a barricade to his flat, and we also hear PiC putting his bike against the balcony railings (lines 02–03). During lines 04–10 N1 comments and cheers PiC on in his move inside away from the balcony. While PiC remains nonverbal (e.g., no "Okay then, I'm coming in"), his eventual cooperation is what the negotiators have been working towards, and which they successfully achieve three and a half hours into the negotiation.

The next case we explore is an emergency call involving a person in crisis who is situated on a bridge threatening to jump. Though it takes considerably shorter time to reach a resolution in Case 2 compared to Case 1, the two cases are similar in that the person in crisis will start showing strong resistance to eventually a weaker resistance, thereby giving the negotiator an opportunity to gain cooperation.

Case 2: "Off the bridge"

Case 2 summary: In this negotiation, the caller is the person in crisis (PiC) and calls the emergency services from the side of a bridge. The dispatcher's primary goal is to get the person in crisis' exact location so she can dispatch police assistance for negotiation. However, this person in crisis refuses to give his location and remains sitting on the side of the bridge with his feet over the edge. The person in crisis reports that he left the hospital without being discharged and has stopped taking his medication for his mental health issues. He claims he had an argument with his girlfriend, who told him to call 911, and that he is scared, sad, and depressed. When the call begins, the person in crisis is on another phone line (presumably with his girlfriend) as the dispatcher answers his call.

In emergency calls where callers threaten self-harm, call takers have two primary goals. The first is to get their specific location so they can send help. The second is getting the person to safety and to choose life. A person in crisis may resist both moving to safety and providing location details. Example 5.4 comes from the very beginning of the call, and we observe the *strongest resistance* in this case towards providing the dispatcher with his location.

```
Example 5.4: Off the bridge
30   DIS:   Who are you talking to:.
31               (.)
```

```
32   PiC:   My fri:end (.) And she's pissin'
33          me off on my other pho:ne I:- she
34          broke my hea:rt y'sterday. I'm on th' edge
35          of th' bridge and I'm fuckin' pissed off.
36   DIS:   What bri:dge.
37              (0.5)
38   PiC:   I can't tell you.
```

We see DIS engage with PiC at line 30 by asking who he is speaking with, and the caller reports that he is on the "edge of the bridge and I'm fuckin' pissed off" (lines 34–35). DIS asks, "What bridge" (line 36) as a way of getting the location information, critical for sending help. However, after half a second of silence (line 37) PiC answers "I can't tell you" (38), which communicates an unwillingness to cooperate (rather than an inability to say or not knowing). Thus, PiC actively creates a barrier for further talk towards the provision of getting help off the bridge.

Like Case 1, PiC shifts from a position of strong resistance to showing signs of *weakening their resistance* to getting help. In the case of "Off the Bridge" near the beginning of the call, PiC indicates that he left the hospital without being formally discharged and that his newly pregnant girlfriend is breaking his heart. In Example 5.5, PiC weakens resistance to his commitment to jump off the bridge by offering a location without specification.

```
Example 5.5: Off the bridge
69   DIS:   Wel[l if  ]yer gunna have a baby yer not
70   PiC:      [Li:ke-]
71   DIS:   gunna kill yerself.
72              (0.2)
73   PiC:   I know bu:hht=huh
74   DIS:   Come on:¿
75              (0.2)
76   DIS:   You gotta (.) enjo:y that.
```

```
77                    (0.2)
78   DIS:   Don't worry about her.
79                    (0.5)
80   PiC:   Well.=hh I'm in Ashforth.=hh
81   DIS:   Where in Ashforth.
82   PiC:   Ah: Don't send th' police.
83   DIS:   Well what do you want from me. (er-)
```

To DIS's suggestion that "well if yer gunna have a baby yer not gunna kill yerself." (line 69), PiC replies, "I know but." (line 72). The "I know" aligns with the call taker's logic for why he should choose life, however the contrastive "but" (line 73) projects a counter to her rationale and marks a form of resistance.

Next, DIS pursues a less resistant answer with "Come on." (line 73). As DIS continues to pursue PiC's agreement through subsequent prompts (lines 75 and 77), PiC offers his location with a town name, "Well. I'm in Ashforth." (line 79). Although PiC retains resistance by not immediately cooperating with DIS's moves, he shows signs of bending towards cooperation by offering his location, yet still resisting help by giving the town without a specific street. We see PiC maintains his line of resistance after DIS asks for a more specific location (line 80), when PiC tells her not to send the police.

Finally, after several minutes of getting PiC to tell his story of what happened prior to his coming to the bridge, DIS again works to persuade PiC to safety. Although dispatchers' primary goal is getting a specific address, we see in this negotiation that DIS makes PiC safety the primary concern as she continues to ask him to get off the side of the bridge by giving him a reason to choose life (line 98).

```
Example 5.6: Off the bridge
98   DIS:   Jus' do us all a favour and get offa th' le:dge.
99                 (1.2)
```

```
100 PiC:    I'm in Corning Stree:t an:d I'm no:t
101         gunna jump I promise.
```

Rather than responding to the directives to move towards safety, PiC offers a more specific location in response, "I'm on Corning Street" with a promise to not jump off the side, "I'm not gunna jump I promise" (line 100–101), thereby resolving the critical life-threatening aspects of the negotiation. We see the success later in the negotiation when PiC agrees to climb over the bridge rail to safety.

The cases above show how people in crisis, in two different negotiations, move from places of strong resistance towards weaker forms of resistance, then finally a crisis resolution. We proceed to ask:

- What exactly happens in between to make these shifts happen?
- How can weaker forms of resistance be used as an opportunity to facilitate resolution?

In the next section we show there are specific interaction techniques that facilitate positive shifts in behaviour, specifically particular types of challenges and the power of leveraging upon the person in crisis' own words. When used productively, these techniques may be as close as we get to having a 'magic wand' to resolve crisis negotiations.

INTERACTIONAL TECHNIQUES TO OVERCOME RESISTANCE

In this section we show how negotiators find opportunities to overcome resistance and facilitate a positive crisis resolution. There are various techniques negotiators use to make these shifts happen. Our research highlights two key interactional techniques:

1. Getting the caller to talk about their stance by asking "why"
2. Using the person in crisis' own words to facilitate a shift in their stance towards the negotiation

Based on Cases 1 and 2 in the previous section, we focus on the sequences of talk leading up to the demonstrable shifts in a person in crisis behaviour. We analyse the interaction to show what is working and how, keeping in mind that one shift in behaviour does not mean that the crisis is resolved. As will be evident in this chapter and the next, the resolution process ebbs and flows, which poses both challenges and opportunities for the negotiators.

We return now to the emergency call, "Off the bridge", introduced in the previous section, and examine how the negotiators get beyond the initial strong resistance against providing location information, to getting the person in crisis to talk.

1. Getting the caller to talk about their stance by asking "why"

PiC has demonstrated a strong form of resistance by responding to DIS's request for the location with "I can't tell you." (line 37). While DIS could pursue a response with another question about the location, she changes her focus to PiC's point of view by asking an open-ended question, "Why:." (line 39).

```
Example 5.7: Off the bridge
37   PiC:  I can't tell you.
38                (0.2)
39   DIS:  Why:.
40                (.)
41   PiC:  Because I'm ma:d.=.hh And I'm sa:d
42         an' I'm heartbroken an' I jus' got
43         outta th' hospital,.hh and she wz there
44         t'visit me this whole time.hh an' now
45         I'm outsi:de uh- heartbroken an' tryin'
46         d'jus kill myself because I'm:
47         just heartbroken..hh An' if you send
48         th' cops I'm just going t'do it anyway.
49                (0.4)
```

```
50   DIS:   .pt.hh Okay=but I don't know where you
51          are so I can't send th' co:ps, just talk
52          to me don't jump.
```

While some training material recommends against asking "why"-type questions (e.g., James, 2008), we find the "why" question is productive for getting people in crisis to talk. In response to the "why" question, PiC answers the question by framing his narrative based on his current emotional state. He labels his emotional state as "mad", "sad", and "heartbroken" (lines 41–42), which provides a framework for how DIS should understand his perspective. PiC offers an account of what happened just prior to going on the bridge, which provides his rationale for being "heartbroken an' tryin d'jus kill myself." (lines 45–46). Here PiC offers his logical rationale for wanting to take his life and gives DIS information for understanding his current stance. PiC ends his narrative by maintaining his resistance to help, thereby keeping the upper hand when he threatens, "if you send th' cops I'm just going t'do it anyway." (lines 47–48). DIS's next turn reassures him that she cannot send the police without the address and instructs him to just talk to her.

In this case the "Why" question succeeds in getting PiC to open up. By using the open-ended "Why" DIS invites PiC to speak to his own agenda, offering information that helps her understand his point of view. PiC's narrative is tied to his agenda for self-harm, yet also gives DIS the background she needs to work with PiC. Next, we see how the negotiator uses PiC's own words as leverage for shifts in attitude or behaviour.

2. Using a person in crisis' own words to facilitate a shift in their stance towards the negotiation

As the call continues, PiC makes a general statement that "everybody always hurts me" and DIS uses this as another opportunity to keep PiC talking about the circumstances leading up to his decision to kill himself. Her next question, "What happened" targets PiC's just prior turn, but narrows the range of what he can provide in response (an account for how people hurt him, for example):

```
Example 5.8: Off the bridge (cont'd)
59   PiC:   I wz- I wz- uh:m in th' hospital b'fore
60          because (.) uh:m I jus' got out two days
61          ago (.) an' uhm an'may- Michael Maywood
62          .hh an'=uhm an' some kid tried t'beat me
63          up the:re and the:n I left
64          >against medical advise< an' I wasn't
65          ready,.hh an' now I got in ( ) my
66          girlfriend.>she wz=uh< brea:k my hea:rt
67          an' then she wz gunna uh:m- she wz gunna
68          uh:m- she wzn't gunna let me kill myself
69          an' now I'm hur:t because (.) I- I care
70          about her an' love her an' she's pregnant
71          with my baby .hh an' now I'm heartbroken
72          and everything.
73   DIS:   Wel[l if  ]yer gunna have a baby yer not
74   PiC:      [Li:ke- ]
75          gunna kill yerself.
76               (0.2)
77   PiC:   I know bu:hht=huh
78   DIS:   Come on:¿
79               (0.2)
80   DIS:   You gotta (.) enjo:y that.
81               (0.2)
82   DIS:   Don't worry about her.
83               (0.5)
84   PiC:   Well.=hh I'm in Ashforth.=hh
85   DIS:   Where in Ashforth.
86   PiC:   Ah: Don't send th' police.
```

Based on PiC response, we find several key pieces of information that provide background as to why PiC is in crisis. He reports someone threatened to harm him (lines 61–62), he left the hospital against medical advice (line 64), and that while his girlfriend has hurt him, she is also pregnant with his child (line 70). In her next turn we see how DIS works to leverage PiCs own words, and components of his agenda for self-harm, to turn the conversation towards agreeing to choose life, "Well if yer gunna have a baby yer not gunna kill yerself." (line 73). Starting her turn with an indirect, "Well" as opposed to sounding more direct, offers a natural upshot to the moral of PiC story and finds the silver lining in his narrative. She ends her turn without further talk, allowing for PiC to agree (or not) with how she understands the outcome. While PiC delays an immediate response (line 76), he starts saying, "I know bu:hht" (line 77), that apparently agrees with DIS's reasoning, yet maintains some resistance towards its implications.

At this point we ask: What could a negotiator do when she can hear PiC bending towards agreeing with her logic? DIS uses this moment as an opportunity to pursue agreement when she coaxes a response with, "Come on:¿" (line 78). While PiC remains silent over the course of the next several turns, DIS continues to pursue agreement with the positive news of having a baby (line 80), and suggests that he remain focused on the baby rather than worrying about his girlfriend (line 82), who PiC indicated was going to end their relationship (line 66). By pursuing PiC's agreement based on his report of what happened, DIS does not directly attempt to resolve the crisis. Instead, she focuses her concern on the logical implications of PiC's words. Through this move, PiC shifts from strong to weak resistance by which he agrees with a positive upshot to his life situation, that having a baby is a reason to choose life.

Although PiC does not explicitly agree with what DIS offered, PiC demonstrates a willingness to ease his resistance by telling her which town he is in, "Well.=.hh I'm in Ashforth." (line 84). With this turn he maintains his autonomy in the encounter and keeps the upper hand by giving a location, but also adding a directive to not send the police (line 86). Thus, PiC is not at risk to compromise his position; meanwhile, the negotiation has moved one step closer towards identifying PiC's location.

While dispatchers orient to their primary agenda of getting a specific location, they suspend getting the location as the primary concern if getting the person to a safe place becomes critical as in the current case. While DIS suspends an explicit pursuit of her agenda, she is able to achieve a successful outcome by remaining focused on PiC's point of view, making use of reasoning based on PiC's own words: specifically, that he is not going to end life given that he is about to become a father.

```
Example 5.9: Off the bridge (cont'd)
91   DIS:  Okay. But *uh* don't you think that yer
92         baby is a good enough reason not t'jump
93         off that bridge.
94              (1.2)
95   PiC:  No:=mh (0.2) Yah: but jus' as an a:hhh uh:
96   DIS:  Wul [get of]fa th' le:dge
97   PiC:      [A'righ]
98              (0.5)
99   DIS:  Jus' do us all a favour and get offa
100        th' le:dge.
101             (1.2)
102  PiC:  I'm in Corning Stree:t an:d I'm no:t
103        gunna jump I promise.
```

Rather than pushing her agenda of getting the location, DIS works to leverage PiC's words and life concerns by designing talk for his agreement, "don't you think that yer baby is a good enough reason not t'jump off that bridge" (lines 92–93). Here DIS appeals to PiC's sense of moral reasoning by proposing that having a baby is a reason to choose life and return to safety. PiC initially tries to maintain his resistance when he says, "No" (line 95), but then in the same turn breaks his resistance with "yah: but" (line 95). In a place where PiC could go on, DIS quickly seizes the opportunity by treating his response as agreement when she says, "well get offa th' le:dge." (line 96). Her move is well placed as it comes immediately following an indication of resistance and moves the call forward by working to get him to safety. Although PiC does not immediately comply in the next turn, DIS continues to work on getting the caller to safety, even pleading, "Jus' do us all a favour and get offa th' le:dge." (line 99). While DIS makes getting off the ledge the relevant move, PiC does not fully comply at this point. However, in response he shows a break in resistance by offering, without further prompting from DIS, a more specific location by giving the name of the street (line 102), and then promises that he will not jump off the bridge (102–103).

So far, we have shown interactional techniques dispatchers use that work towards overcoming resistance and getting PiC to safety.

LESSONS FROM "OFF THE BRIDGE"

- Asking wh-questions like "Why?" and targeted wh-questions like "what happened?" work to invite a person in crisis's narrative about what led them to their current situation. Through these narratives, negotiators invite the person in crisis to offer their own perspective in a non-threatening manner.
- Focusing on the person in crisis' agenda by asking questions that get at their point of view and life concerns enable them to talk about the reasons that brought them to *their* own decision-making processes.
- Suspending the organizational agenda (e.g., getting the person in crisis' address) and focusing on the person in crisis' agenda weakens their resistance.

In the next section we explore what characterizes interactional challenges that work in making a productive negotiation with a person in crisis.

WHEN INTERACTIONAL CHALLENGES WORK TO OVERCOME RESISTANCE

An interactional challenge can support a positive rather than a negative turning point in the person in crisis's behaviour, by producing a demonstrable shift in their stance towards the negotiation.

Similar to Case 2, "Off the bridge", the negotiator in Case 1, "Off the balcony", challenges PiC's resistance using "their own terms", which becomes a key moment in the negotiation (see also Sikveland et al., 2020).

In Example 5.10, N initiates a proposal whereby he offers PiC a cigarette in exchange for taking the noose off his neck (lines 01–02). Taking the noose off would eliminate the immediate threat, and possibly move PiC into a safer territory for subsequent negotiation. We focus on how N identifies and leverages upon a logical consequence of PiC's resistant response.

```
Example 5.10: Take off noose
01   N:    In exchange for getting you a cigarette
02         over there, (0.6) can you take that noose
03         off from round your neck please.
04              (1.6)
05   N:    Will [you do th-    ]
06   PiC:       [It won't make a] difference.
07              (0.8)
08   N:    Well if it doesn't make a difference,
09         Take it off then.
10              (2.3)
11   PiC:  But why would I take it off though.
```

The negotiator's proposal (lines 01–02) is initially met with a long 1.6 seconds of silence (line 03), which forecasts PiC's possible trouble with agreeing to his terms. The negotiator then pursues the proposal (line 05), but before he completes his turn, PiC starts in overlap by rejecting the N's terms, "It won't make a difference."' (line 06).

Crucially, while PiC's use of "it" indexes the act of taking off the noose, this pronoun also implies that removing the noose would not change his intentions. After the silence at line 06, N works to undermine PiC's rejection by expanding the sequence and using his turn as a resource for building our target challenge in the next turn, "Well if it doesn't make a difference, Take it off then."

(lines 08–09). N thereby challenges PiC using PiC's own words, as it were, against him.

Does the negotiator's challenge make a difference to the PiC's decision to keep the noose on or off? Initially, instead of taking the noose off, PiC asks for an account, with "But why would I take it off though." (line 11). The negotiator could have answered it's because he's worried, or because something terrible might happen. But instead, the negotiator sticks to his counter-argument: "Well you've just said to me it doesn't make a difference." (lines 13–14) and thereby pursues his request for PiC to remove the noose, in order to receive his cigarette.

```
Example 5.11: Take off noose (cont'd)
12                 (0.2)
13  N:     Well you've just said to me it
14         doesn't make a difference.
15                 (1.8)
16  N:     In which case take it off.
17                 (5.2)
18  N:     Okay?
19                  (.)
20  N:     <As soon as we find a lighter.=
21         We'll have the cigarette here.
22         But I want you to take the noose off:
23         (0.7) before I pass it over.
24                 (0.2)
25  N:     Okay,
26                 (1.3)
27  PiC:   I'll still be right up at the edge,
28         (0.4) It don't make damn bit of difference.=
29         You see me take it off? (0.2) I'll put it
30         right back on. Cos I'll keep it right
           here.
```

Following an extended silence and the negotiator pursuing an answer (lines 15–26), PiC finally removes the noose around line 27. PiC even uses the argument "it won't make a difference" to his own favour. From his perspective, PiC 'wins' the argument by maintaining his stance, while in effect complying to what the negotiator asked him to do. PiC argues he can put the noose on whenever he likes to, and this is something that the negotiator can easily agree with without risking PiC harming himself. The result is a productive use of a challenge that leads to PiC moving away from immediate harm.

We can see how challenges work in Example 5.12; this time a "why don't you"-type format pushes for agreement. While in and of itself "why don't you" might not sound like a promising technique for dealing with strong resistance, in this case it contributes towards influencing PiC's behaviour.

```
Example 5.12: Sit on another bit
01   N1:    You've got all control over there,
02          That whole roof is yours.
03              (.)
04   N1:    We're not coming up there, (.) so why do
05          you got to sit on that bit.
06              (6.6)
07   N1:    Why don't you go and sit (.) on another bit.
08              (3.6)
09   N1:    Sit at the other end.=Where you can
10          speak to (d-) (0.2) Kathy.
11              (0.5)
12   N2:    °Y:es:::°
```

N1 promotes a reason why PiC should move based on "control": "You've got all control over there," (line 01) and "The whole roof is yours." (line 02). N also reassures PiC that the negotiators are not going to intervene, "We're not coming up there," (line 04). Based on this form of reasoning, N1 then proposes PiC moves to "another" part of the roof "(lines 04–07). This part of the roof is also closer to a member of the negotiation team with whom PiC has previously engaged, hence the reference to "Kathy" (lines 9–10). PiC moves towards that end, which the secondary negotiator orients to in line 12.

WHEN INTERACTIONAL CHALLENGES DO NOT WORK TO OVERCOME RESISTANCE

To facilitate influence over PiC, negotiators can use power-terms such as "control", but it must be used at the right time. In 5.12, we see how the negotiator uses the term "control" to give PiC the agency to move to a safer part of the roof. But, as with telling a PiC what to do in general, framing its reasoning on "control" does not work in and by itself. Example 5.13 from the same negotiation demonstrates this point.

```
Example 5.13: You can stop this
01   N:      But you can stop this. Can't you.
02   PiC:    No.=
03   N:      =You're- you can stop this:.
04              (0.2)
05   N:      You are comple:tely in contro:l.
06              (0.3)
07   N:      You can stop this.=You can come do:wn.
08              (2.2)
09   PiC:    No.
10              (0.2)
11   PiC:    I'm not coming down.
12              (6.5)
13   PiC:    I hope you get paid good overtime.
```

Unlike the (interactionally) irrefutable reasoning we presented earlier, N's "you can come do:wn" (line 07) is not built out of a logical reasoning that preserves PiC's autonomy. N has not set up the local context that would warrant coming down as the irrefutable reasoned consequence of PiC's own words.

The take-home message is not that any kind of challenge works. When reasoning is based on their own words, these are particular, well-reasoned challenges that are very hard for the person in crisis to reject. This point is further illuminated in cases where the negotiator poses a challenge, but it leads to an escalation of the resistance rather than alleviating it. Example 5.14 shows that without some form of reasoning built off PiC's words or agenda, asking PiC to do something that contributes towards keeping them safe can easily be outright rejected.

```
Example 5.14: I'm not sitting down
01  N:      Please sit down safely.=I don't want
02          you to hurt yourself.
03                (0.4)
04  PiC:    Where.
05                (0.9)
06  N:      Well just sit down where you are.=
07  PiC:    =I'm not SITTING DOWN!
08                (0.8)
09  N:      Okay well stand still then.=That-
10  PiC:    NO:!
11                (.)
12  N:      You're very high up there.
13                (0.3)
14  PiC:    No I'm not standing still:, (.) I'm not sitting do:wn,
15                (0.5)
16  PiC:    I'm doing it.
```

N formulates a request, "Please sit down safely." (line 01) and gives the account that he does not want PiC to "hurt yourself." (lines 01–02). It seems initially that, after the silence at line 03, PiC is willing to find a seat, as he asks, "Where." (line 04). But after N suggests, sit "where you are." (line 06), PiC yells, thereby resisting and rejecting the request (lines 07, 10 and 14). The example ends with an explicit threat that PiC is "doing it." (line 16; PiC elaborates on this threat in his subsequent talk). While we have seen a "well"-prefaced argument contribute to a positive behaviour shift elsewhere (see Example 5.11), it only works to escalate the resistance in Example 5.14: there is no well-reasoned interactional challenge supporting the negotiator's request for PiC to move to safety.

What makes the failed attempts (Examples 5.13 and 5.14) *refutable* is the reverse reason the positive cases (Examples 5.10–5.12) are *irrefutable*: the former do not leverage logical reasoning. Also, they occur early in the negotiation and might ask for 'too much' too soon. So where and how do people in crisis draw the line between what is and isn't 'too much', and for the negotiation, 'too risky'? Part of the answer to this comes with our final example in this chapter.

Example 5.15 is, like Examples 5.10–12, taken from a later stage of the negotiation, but unlike the earlier examples it shows how N initially produces a productive challenge but fails to leverage it. This comes an hour into a different negotiation, where PiC is barricaded in her flat, standing on a chair with a noose around her neck. The negotiators are in the corridor outside PiC's flat, and N can see her through locked grille doors. We focus on what happens after PiC agrees that her suicide does not have to happen yet (lines 07–09).

```
Example 5.15: It doesn't have to happen yet
01  N:       And just stand- ↑or put both feet back on
02           the (t-) chair for a start, (.) just do
03           that at least. Please.
04                 (1.0)
05  PiC:     No,=it's happening.
06                 (1.2)
07  N:       It doesn't have to happen yet though does it.
08                 (0.2)
09  PiC:     °No°,
10  N:       It doesn't< have to happen.
```

```
11              [>It doesn't have to<] happen at all.
12  PiC:    [ (mm:)                        ]
13  PiC:    Yeah it does,
```

N's proposal that "It doesn't have to happen yet though does it." (line 07) acts like a challenge, highlighting a flaw in PiC's account that "it's happening" (line 05). In this way, the N does not challenge PiC's choice to take their own life but challenges its imminence. At line 09, PiC agrees with N's proposal. The '°No°,' is produced quietly following a 0.2 second gap, and might thereby project a reservation towards a stronger form of agreement. At the same time, this is an opportunity to productively leverage the challenge posed in line 07. However, N misses the opportunity to do so, and PiC's next response (line 13) is a strong rejection of PiC's next move (lines 10–11). In his next turn, N first redoes what PiC already agreed to – "It doesn't have to happen." (line 10). Then, in the same turn, he redoes what he did before by upgrading with an extreme case formulation (Edwards, 2000), "at all" at the end: "It doesn't have to happen at all." (line 11). By redoing what he already did (and what PiC already agreed to), but in absolute terms (not doing it at all), N opens opportunities for rejection and an escalation of the crisis, which is what happens in line 13 when PiC responds, "Yeah it does," (line 13). Following this extract, PiC starts kicking the chair she is on and thereby increases the risk of her falling off it; after extended and escalated threats of suicide, PiC eventually gives the negotiators the keys to her door and they get her safely down. What we observe here is how a reasoned consequence can change from irrefutable to refutable with one turn of talk, which may have long-term consequences for the negotiation.

Resistance ebbs and flows, and resistance is a resource for negotiators to use and leverage upon to facilitate small steps towards a resolution. We explore this point further in Chapter 6.

SUMMARY

Negotiation is not a straightforward and linear task. Resistance ebbs and flows, but we show there are ways resistance is a resource for gradually facilitating the person in crisis' independent decision to choose life. In the end, the goal is

> **TAKEAWAY PRACTICAL STRATEGIES: OVERCOME RESISTANCE**
>
> - The challenge of keeping the conversation going is managed turn by turn. Avoid pushing too far, too soon.
> - Challenges ("why"); imperatives ("take it off") are effective when based in the person in crisis's own terms and logic.
> - People in crisis demonstrate an apparent unwillingness to present themselves as unreasonable or irrational. This is a resource for negotiators in order to overcome resistance.

not for the person in crisis to comply, but for them to CHOOSE life, independently from the negotiator's agenda. The shifts observed in this chapter are all significant in terms of the professional's (negotiator or dispatcher) goals to ensure the person in crisis is safe.

REFERENCES

Cooper, H. T. (2007). Decision making in a crisis. *Journal of Police Crisis Negotiations, 7*(2), 5–28.

Edwards, D. (2000). Extreme case formulations: Softeners, investment, and doing nonliteral. *Research on Language and Social Interaction, 33*(4), 347–373.

Ireland, C. A., & Vecchi, G. M. (2009). The Behavioral Influence Stairway Model (BISM): a framework for managing terrorist crisis situations? *Behavioral Sciences of Terrorism and Political Aggression, 1*(3), 203–218.

James, R. K. (2008). *Crisis intervention strategies.* Belmont, CA: Thomson Brooks/Cole.

McMains, M., & W. Mullins. 2014. *Crisis negotiations: Managing critical incidents and hostage situations in law enforcement and corrections.* New York: Routledge.

Sikveland, R. O., Kevoe-Feldman, H., & Stokoe, E. (2020). Overcoming suicidal persons' resistance using productive communicative challenges during police crisis negotiations. *Applied Linguistics, 41*(4), 533–551.

'Coming down' Scaffolding a resolution to the crisis

Chapter 6

DOI: 10.4324/9780429354892-6

WHAT IS THIS CHAPTER ABOUT?

As we began to discuss at the start of the previous chapter, persons in crisis do not simply *agree* to 'come down' if and when a negotiator or call taker asks them to do so. They *decide* to do so. Put another way, although the professional parties negotiate with persons in crisis, and are, of course, co-constructing its outcome turn-by-turn, the key to resolution is enabling the person in crisis to talk about things they have decided to do and will decide to do, not *agree* to do. This chapter returns to the key concepts of agency and control, fundamental to how people in crisis resist the negotiation, and how they eventually move towards safety.

We ask:

What characterizes circumstances in which persons in crisis decide to come down safely?

WHY IS THIS TOPIC IMPORTANT?

Managing conflict and creating the interactional foundations for resolution is key to successful crisis negotiations. In Chapter 5, we saw how negotiation is a process that 'ebbs and flows', meaning that while a demonstrable shift in behaviour may not resolve the crisis, it can be a step in the right direction. However, a step in the wrong direction can easily occur. It can be useful to think of negotiations using a 'spiral' metaphor: at the top of the spiral is the person in crisis, the negotiator or call-taker, and life, and at the bottom of the crisis is the person in crisis, the negotiator or call-taker, and death. Across the negotiation, the person in crisis moves up and down the spiral.

Effective negotiation involves setting up the conditions for – or scaffolding – the person in crisis to actively articulate a decision to come down. Understanding how to mobilize the person in crisis' autonomy productively is, therefore, a key resource for negotiators. Our research identifies practices that show how negotiators do this scaffolding, autonomy-boosting work, while promoting safe decisions to come down.

WHAT CURRENT TRAINING TELLS US ABOUT SCAFFOLDING THE PERSON IN CRISIS'S DECISION TO 'COME DOWN'

Two primary themes in-and phases of-negotiation training are relationship-building and problem-solving. Problem-solving is regarded as central to resolving conflict and moving towards resolution (Oostinga, Giebels, & Taylor, 2018; Vecchi, Van Hasselt, & Romano, 2005), especially when it builds on achievements in relationship-building. Training, therefore, points to relationship-building as one of the elements leading up to the positive resolution of the negotiation:

> The emphasis on the relationship-building process highlights the importance of having a positive and trusting relationship between the perpetrator and negotiator if behavioral change and peaceful resolution are to take place.
>
> (Ireland & Vecchi, 2009, p. 207)

Building a positive relationship with a person in crisis is thus seen as the holy grail for successful outcomes. Since positive relationships are connected to trust, training suggests communication modalities and behaviour to calm the situation, such as supportive and engaging talk about a positive future or outcome (Miller, 2005) to send the message to the person in crisis that a situation is salvageable, and that something can be done to remedy the crisis.

While the person in crisis and the negotiator may have different goals during an encounter, there are areas of common interest that serve as a foundation for relationship building and for positive problem-solving outcomes. Negotiators should identify what those are and engage a person in crisis in the decision-making process related to his/her fate (Mullins, 2002). Current training on problem-solving emphasizes principles of persuasion behind getting agreement and compliance from the person in crisis (Mullins, 2002, building on Ury, 1991 and "getting past the 'no'"), and central to negotiation is getting a commitment from the person in crisis through consistent communication to allow for positive choices (McMains & Mullins, 2014). However, Ireland and Vecchi (2009) warn:

> An over-emphasis on problem-solving can lead a negotiator to potentially focus too heavily on seeking the motivation behind the crisis, which may potentially lead to a tendency to rush the perpetrator to resolution.
>
> (Ireland & Vecchi, 2009, p. 207)

To describe methods for getting a person in crisis to move towards a positive choice, and towards safety, we use the term 'scaffolding'. Used in education (Hogan & Pressley, 1997) and crisis resolution, 'scaffolding' is the visual representation of the STEPS model (see Kelln & McMurtry, 2007). Scaffolding captures the supportive features for *making* a decision, rather than forcing or coercing a *decision* (or *learning* in educational contexts). The scaffolding concept fits with the relationship building models such as Behavioural Influence Stairway Model (BISM), and STEPS.

However, little is known about the methods for actually achieving this practice in and through the interactions. For example, training may overlook how relationship issues typically drive conflict and problem-solving from the start of encounters. Thus, we find a gap in training for understanding how to synthesize relationship-building and problem-solving as part of the negotiation.

WHAT DO DECISIONS TO 'COME DOWN' LOOK LIKE?

It is common for people in crisis to use strong forms of resistance, which are characteristic of crisis negotiation. Our first example might surprise some, however, because the person in crisis apparently comes down simply in response to a plea from the negotiator:

```
Example 6.1: Coming down [1 hr 49 mins into the
negotiation]
01   N1:     We really want you to come down buddy.
02   PiC:    Coming down.
```

In line 01, the negotiator (N1) asserts their interest in PiC coming down and, without delay, PiC answers, "Coming down." (line 02). In the next moments (not shown), PiC does indeed come down safely from the roof -they are not referring to a suicidal jump. Is it really this easy? Example 6.1 occurs after 1 hour and 49 minutes into the negotiation, after an extended and stepwise negotiation up until this point. There is more information in these two turns than perhaps meets the reader's eye at first, and we return to this example at the end of the current section to explain.

In this chapter, we explore how negotiators achieve such a seemingly straightforward resolution. First, we look at some other instances in which the person in crisis comes down safely. Example 6.2 is a case where the person in crisis is on a balcony, and the negotiator (N1) works on getting them to a safer place.

```
Example 6.2: Off the balcony
01   N1:    Okay¿ All they want- (0.8) is for you to
02          be safe warm and dry.
03                  (2.0)
04   N1:    Yeah?
05                  (1.5)
06   N1:    Good ma:n.
07                  (0.6) / ((sounds of bike being
08          put up against railings))
09   N1:    That's it.
10                  (0.3)
11   N1:    Stand it up there,
12                  (0.7)
13   N1:    Very well done.=Now if you open that door¿
14                  (0.6)
15   N1:    Go in,
16                  (1.4)
17          ((Crowd cheers))
18   N1:    I wanna go. I wanna go through.
19                  (5.5) / ((N1 moves towards PiC's flat))
```

At line 01, the negotiator seeks to minimize the significance of PiC moving to a safer place by saying, "All they want– (0.8) is for you to be safe warm and dry.", which focuses on the physical move and not the bigger picture related to reasons for being on the balcony. After a delay at line 03, PiC says "Yeah?" before making the first move to coming down at lines 05–07, to which N1 says, "Good maːn." (line 06). PiC moves inside his flat around line 15 (in response to which the bystanders cheer, line 16–17). We highlight PiC's move to safety comes without an explicit verbal agreement to coming down. He carries out his move towards safety himself.

Similarly, in the next example, we see PiC moving towards safety without verbalizing the action.

Example 6.3: Watch your step [1 hr 40 mins into the negotiation]

```
01   N1:      Will you come doːwn.
02            (1.5)
03   N2:      Watch your step mate,
04            (0.3)
05   N2:      Watch your step.
```

In cases where PiC verbalizes their effort to move to safety, PiC does not directly comply with the negotiator's request. Rather, they make clear they are coming down of their own volition. Example 6.4 is one such example, from an emergency 911 call where PiC is sitting on the edge of a bridge, prepared to jump.

Example 6.4: Off the bridge

```
141  DIS:     Soː how 'bout you jus' get offa thaːt¿
142            (0.2)
143  PiC:     What about if I cliːmb over:. on thee
144           other side of th' sidewaːlk.
```

While DIS's request, "So: how 'bout you jus' get offa tha:t"
(line 141) could get an agreement in the form of an "okay then",
or "yes I will," PiC offers an independent suggestion, "What about
if I cli:mb over: on thee other side of th' sidewa:lk." While DIS's
turn gives a prompt or suggestion, we again see a silence (line
142) before PiC initiates a move that appears separate from the
negotiator's demands.

Returning to Example 6.1, we can notice a condensed but
similar form to the above cases.

```
Example 6.1: Coming down
01  N1:     We really want you to come down buddy.
02  PiC:    Coming down.
```

In each of the cases (Examples 6.2–6.4), the persons in crisis
avoid direct agreement or compliance with their negotiators.
In Example 6.1, "coming down" is not an explicit agreement
to the negotiator's proposal, such as, "yes I will" or "okay
then". However, notice that PiC uses a grammatical form that
communicates an independent move; that is, coming down is
based on PiC's decision and not by virtue of the negotiator's
prompt. While it is not immediately evident that PiC *decides*, as
opposed to agreeing, to come down, it is nevertheless evident
when we look at the grammar of the response. The grammar
of 'deciding' becomes especially illuminating when PiC seems
to be complying, but is doing so in his own terms, and as self-
initiated, "(I'm) coming down".

The next example provides further insight into, and evidence
for, the 'scaffolding' of persons in crisis' independent decisions
as an effective strategy. We join the conversation after a
person in crisis has come down and agreed to be taken to an
assessment centre. But prior to line 01, he starts backtracking
by asking N to confirm that he is not going to change these
arrangements.

```
Example 6.5: Winding me up
01  N:      There's no need for me to break
```

```
02            any promises, (0.8) uhthm
03                 (6.6)
04  N:        We can think about going to that
05            Spurs game next season.
06                 (17.1)
07  N:        A:nd looking at that course >to help<
08            (0.6) children like your mum does.
09                 (1.3)
10  N:        She's obviously a loving lady isn't
11            she. Helping all those children,
12                 (10.3)
13  PiC:      See you you're winding me up now
14            you're making me change my mi(h)nd.
15  N:        <Why?>
16                 (0.5)
17  PiC:      Well like asking me about Spurs
18            games (and) ((inaudible due to noise))
19  N:        Huhuh £why£ is that.
20                 (0.5)
21  PiC:      It's just winding me u:p.
```

Lines 01–18 feature the negotiator claiming (lines 01–02) and then demonstrating (lines 04–05 and 07–08) that he is committed to keeping the promises he had made to PiC which had led PiC to announce that he would come down from the rooftop. With no engagement from PiC (notice the long gaps at lines 03, 06, and 09), N changes tack, praising PiC's mum in pursuit of a response from him (lines 10–11). After another long silence (line 12), PiC announces that he is in the course of reverting his commitment to coming down. He uses N's prior actions, which are ostensibly "winding him up" (lines 13 and 21), as the cause. By attributing the responsibility for the change in plans to the negotiator, PiC maintains the appearance of integrity despite reversing his position. PiC also pre-empts further attempts from N to get him to come down by implying that N's actions have been upsetting him. This places N in an unfortunate position because he has inadvertently deterred PiC from coming down.

In other work, we have shown that, by examining how people actually use words like "persuade" and "change your mind" in natural language, "changing one's mind" maintains an agency that "being persuaded" does not (Humă, Stokoe, & Sikveland, 2020). The most productive route to influence is ensuring that people maintain their integrity and agency despite reversing their position. Persuading others can seem to infringe their right to make autonomous decisions, while changing a person's mind, even as a result of another's influence – in this case, the negotiator or call-taker – enables the person in crisis to display autonomy.

LESSONS LEARNED FROM THE CHAPTER SO FAR

- A person in crisis does not agree to come down – they *decide* to come down, and these are the decisions to build towards and look for.
- Negotiators productively allow for silence between their directive or request and the person in crisis's move.
- Agreement from a person in crisis comes in the form of nonverbal moves (the act of coming down) and verbal agreements that explicate their action.

In the next section, we examine how negotiators support, or scaffold, the persons in crisis's decision to come down. Since these moves come over the course of many turns, we point out how this process ebbs and flows between moving from strong reasons not to move to reasons to move.

UP AND DOWN THE NEGOTIATION SPIRAL:
A CASE STUDY

As we noted in Chapter 5, negotiations with a person in crisis are long, with success realized over the course of hours. We also note these negotiations require careful attention to what happens across much smaller units of time, turn by turn. This means that a positive step can spin into a negative step in the next turn of talk. A challenge in crisis talk is to minimize the likelihood for the latter to happen. In what follows, we look at a series of systematic local consequences, based on how proposals are formulated, and how to keep the person in crisis at the spiral's middle-top.

In Chapter 5, we showed how success in the form of some agreement from the person in crisis, may be followed by strong disagreement, from one turn to the next. We see this occurs in Example 6.6, lines 09 and 13, respectively.

```
Example 6.6: It doesn't have to happen yet
01   N1:     And just stand- ↑or put both feet back on
02           the (t-) chair for a start, (.) just do
03           that at least. Please.
04                    (1.0)
05   PiC:    No,=it's happening.
06                    (1.2)
07   N1:     It doesn't have to happen yet though does it.
08                    (0.2)
09   PiC:    °No°,
10   N1:     It doesn't< have to happen.
11           [>It doesn't have to<] happen at all.
12   PiC:    [ (mm:)                ]
13   PiC:    Yeah it does,
```

PiC rejects N1's suggestion of how to move to safety (lines 01–03), "No,=it's happening." (line 05). In an attempt to buy time and keep PiC from carrying out the threat, N1 works to get PiC to hold off, "It doesn't have to happen yet though does it" (line 07), where the last bit, "does it" is designed to get PiC's agreement with the proposal to wait. After the silence at line 08, PiC quietly agrees, "No". To leverage the agreement, the negotiator pushes that proposal (lines 10–11), but pushes too far too soon. PiC is unwilling to agree that the attempted suicide does not need to happen at all, just willing to concede it does not have to happen yet. PiC agrees to holding off, without making a commitment to move to safety or to jump in this moment.

The movement up and down the spiral can be observed from one turn to the next, and also across longer sequences of talk. In emergency call centres, where the average call is about a minute and a half, self-harm calls such as the "Off the bridge" case can run for a half an hour or longer. Our point is that success does not happen immediately, and negotiators must remain alert, turn by turn, and recognize the interaction's ebb and flow. We continue our case study "Off the bridge" (see Chapter 5) and show how there are identifiable moments where traces of resistance exist, even after the person in crisis shows indications of choosing life and moving to safety. And eventually, the person in crisis *does* decide to move to safety.

Example 6.7 comes after the moment PiC offered a street name and promised to remain safe (lines 100–101). Notice how PiC still exhibits signs of resistance after DIS offers to send the police to help him (lines 102–103).

```
Example 6.7: Off the bridge
100   PiC:   I'm in Corning Stree:t an:d I'm no:t
101          gunna jump I promise.
102   DIS:   Okay. So whadda want me t'do. Do you
103          want me t'send th' p'lice there.
104          Do you need [t'go- ]
105   PiC:              [No=ho.] [ N o=h o h ]
106   DIS:                       [Okay. A'righ']
107          Listen. I wo:n't. I won't..hh Do you
108          need [t'go ba:ck t' th' hospital?      ]
109   CLR:        [I'm jus' sittin' here on th' ledge]
110          an' I'm gunna sta:y he:re.
111                   (0.2)
112   CLR:   I'm gunna sta:y here on thee edge.
```

Although PiC indicates cooperation, we see DIS's orientation to the possibility that PiC remains resistant. At line 102, in a place where she could say she's going to send help, she gives PiC the autonomy to make that decision when she asks, "Okay. So whadda want me t'do. Do you want me t'send th' p'lice there. Do you need t'go–" (lines 103–104). However, we see that PiC resists the implication of what the offer means and immediately cries out, "No=ho. No=hoh" (line 105). As an alternative to sending the police, DIS asks if he needs to go back to the hospital (lines 107–108), which he rejects in the next turn by declaring that he will remain on the ledge of the bridge (line 112). While remaining on the ledge is a here and now choice to live, PiC stands his ground by rejecting help and remaining on the bridge. Such moments may cause a negotiator to get stuck as to what they can do next. In this case, DIS asks another open-ended, "Why" (not shown) to get PiC to talk, giving him a slot to explain why he wants to remain on the bridge. In response, he says he finds it peaceful and has no intention of climbing down.

Crisis negotiation training argues that good negotiators need a high level of emotional intelligence. In Example 6.8 we show what such emotional intelligence may look like in an interaction. We present DIS's next move in the "Off the bridge" case, where she displays a high degree of emotional intelligence when she articulates PiC's current state of mind as a reason for him to step off the bridge.

```
Example 6.8: Off the bridge (cont'd)
115  DIS:  Wul I don't think tha:t the edge, is a
116        good place for you right now cuz yer not
117        really too sta:ble.
118             (0.8)
119  PiC:  An' I'm off ov' my me:ds.[ An:d-eh:]
120  DIS:                           [.pt Well.]
121        That's another reason not t'be on the edge.
122        Right?
123  PiC:  An' I ha:d a sei:zure earlier, (.) an'
```

```
124          [u h m:]
125  DIS:    [O:kay.] Wul. It sounds like t'- it
126          sounds like t'me >that you need t'go
127          ba:ck t'th hospita:l.<
```

The ability to recognize and describe PiC's current state of mind without using a negative emotional label (e.g., "you're hysterical", or "you sound upset") displays a higher level of emotional intelligence by communicating her independent understanding of his situation. She conveys an empathetic stance towards his position when she offers an account for why she thinks the edge is not the right place for him to remain, "cuz yer not really too sta:ble" (lines 116–117). While such a stance seems risky, DIS has established a positive relationship with PiC throughout the encounter. PiC opened up about his situation and his problems. She designs an assessment as her concern for his well-being, rather than part of a more authoritarian organizational agenda.

DIS's strategy works to shift PiC away from resistance as he aligns with her assessment by adding information that supports how he's "not too stable." First, he offers another component to what she started when he says, "An, I'm off ov' my meds" (line 119), which provides additional evidence (from his perspective) to support her assessment as correct. DIS uses this new information to get PiC to agree that coming off the bridge is a reasonable option, ".pt Well. That's another reason not t'be on the edge. Right?" (lines 120–121). Designing her turn for confirmation with "right" (line 122), DIS works to gain PiC's commitment to move to safety. While PiC seems primed to agree, he offers additional support that DIS is right about his instability when he admits to having a seizure earlier (line 123). DIS remains on her plan for getting the caller help, but rather than propose sending the police, she suggests going back to the hospital as an alternative (lines 125–127).

PiC's collaboration marks another shift in the negotiation from reporting what happened to explaining his problems. DIS's careful assessment, based on PiC's words, correctly identifies his underlying problem. By offering additional information about his state of mind that builds upon (opposed to countering) DIS's assessment, we see DIS and PiC closing the gap of resistance between them. DIS's effort to gain PiCs commitment to choosing life is followed by PiC's independent decision to climb over the railing to safety.

```
Example 6.8: Off the bridge (cont'd)
135  DIS: But yih know
136       when yer mind switches t'wanting t' jump
137       again you shouldn't be nea:r it.
138            (.)
139  DIS: Yih kno:w. Don't you think that would help?
140  PiC: Yea:h.
141  DIS: So: how 'bout you jus' get offa tha:t¿
142            (0.2)
143  PiC: What about if I cli:mb over:. on thee other
144       side of th' sidewa:lk.
```

After continued resistance to going to the hospital, DIS uses what we call irrefutable logic, a proposal based on something PiC said prior, that is hard for PiC to counter or deny. Drawing from what PiC told her about being off his medication and feeling unstable, she says, "but yih know when yer mind switches t'wanting t'jump again you shouldn't be nea:r it." (lines 135–137). After a beat of silence where PiC could speak next, she prompts him for agreement with, "Yih kno:w. Don't you think that would help?" (line 139). Without delay, PiC immediately agrees, and with a little encouragement (line 141), PiC commits climbing over the railing towards safety.

LESSONS LEARNED FROM EXAMPLES 6.5–6.8

- Agreement is made through small moves over the course of several turns. Scaffolding happens moment to moment, without focusing on the big picture.
- Persons in crisis lean towards showing moves towards 'coming down' as an independent decision based on good will but not a result of the negotiation.

STRATEGIES NEGOTIATORS USE TO 'SPEED UP' THE DECISION-MAKING PROCESS

Once negotiators establish a foundation with the person in crisis, strategies that training deems risky or confrontational work to accelerate the negotiation to a beneficial resolution. Building a scaffolding gives negotiators resources to work within the boundaries of the person in crisis's resistance, thereby creating a positive relationship that allows for trust; and taking some risk. In the case of "Off the balcony" (Examples 6.6–6.8), the negotiator has an understanding of PiC's motive for standing on the balcony and identifies an opportune moment to encourage PiC to come down. In Example 6.9, the negotiator is at the early stages of problem-solving, addressing PiC's means of getting to the loft where he is currently at.

```
Example 6.9: I used to climb up here when I was
little
01   N:      How- how would you- how did you get up
02           here.='n how how will you (k-) (.)
03           sort of get down from here.
04                (2.3)
05   N:      [Did-  ]
06   PiC:    [I used] to climb up here when I was
07           little.
```

One method for getting someone to come down is saying, "come down off the balcony". However, our research shows that recipients can easily reject directives, and what the negotiator is doing instead is to ask a hypothetical question. N asks, "How did you get up here.='n how how will you (k–) (.) sort of get down from here" (lines 01–03). This question sets up a puzzle for PiC to solve. N's turn design also places the solution to the puzzle in PiC's domain of knowledge, casting them as the expert on getting down from this particular location. For 2.3 seconds, there is no answer (line 04), before N and PiC simultaneously initiate the next turn. N pulls out as PiC answers the question. When PiC speaks, he shares that climbing to the loft was something he did as a child (lines 06–07). Sharing something from his past gives N insight about PiC's domain of knowledge, which N can tie to the present situation. N uses PiC's response as a foundation for the next question, focusing on the act of coming down. N orients to practical concerns over using a directive, basing the next turn on the logic that if PiC routinely climbed up there as a child, they should know how to climb down without effort.

We see the negotiators use the person in crisis's sole access to knowledge about practical concerns in our next example also. Here, PiC is on a roof-top, and it is less than obvious how he made it up there in the first place. N is positioned on the ground next to the building.

```
Example 6.10: Hard to get down
01   N:        Is there a way for you to get down there,
02   PiC:      I don't kno:w,
03                     (1.1)
04   PiC:      I've ne- I've not been here,
05                     (0.6)
06   PiC:      ( ) (down here),
07                     (0.4)
08   N:        Cos they look too hard to get down.
```

To speed up the negotiation, N designs a question that prompts PiC to consider coming down. The interest is on how N designs the question as an unknowing party by asking, "Is there a way for you to get down there" (line 01), leaving it up to PiC to explain the route to safety. Rather than using a directive that pre-figures knowing how PiC should climb down, N leaves it in PiC's domain, thereby giving them the autonomy for the next move. Initially, PiC resists the implication of the question by claiming a lack of knowledge, "I don't know" (line 02). The "I don't know" is a move towards agreement but remains within the range of weak forms of resistance, as seen in Chapter 5. Also, we see PiC does not reject the implication of N's question about coming down. Rather, PiC gives an account for not knowing how to get down ("I've not been here" line 04).

In actual negotiation encounters, we find opportunities for action which are missed in training. For example, PiC in Example 6.10 is not refusing or rejecting the idea of coming down. The problem is in the logistics of *how* to get down, thereby creating an opening for pursuing the task of figuring a way out. In Example 6.10, N treats PiC's response as a request for help with figuring out the task, and responds by agreeing with PiC that the route is not straightforward.

As the exchange continues, N builds on the relevance for finding a useful path down and asks PiC directly, "Have you s– (.) found out a way to get down or not." (Example 6.11, line 19). This seems a risky move, and one that PiC pushes back on, "anybody comes I'm jumping" (line 23), after initially having aligned with it, "I'm looking," (line 21). But in this instance, N staves off further rejection by reassuring PiC that nobody is approaching.

```
Example 6.11: A way to get down
19   N:      Have you s- (.) found out a way to get
20           down or not.
21   PiC:    I'm looking,
22                  (0.5)
23   PiC:    A- anybody comes I'm jumping.
24   N:      No one's gonna come. It's gonna be me
25           and you.
```

When a situation turns to a stalemate, negotiators approach the situation from PiC's domain by turning the tables and asking for PiC help. For example, in 6.12, following on from the case presented in Examples 6.10–11, the negotiators attempt to situate a 'cherry picker' (a hydraulic crane with a railed platform for raising and lowering people) by the roof to facilitate PiC's coming down. In response to PiC's rejection of getting on the lift, N declares they are coming up to bring PiC down. Our focus is on what N says to position PiC for rescuing and taking responsibility for a safe journey down.

```
Example 6.12: You'll have to hold me
01   N:      Right. I- I'm gonna come u:p, (0.6) In
```

```
02              that crane. And I'm gonna bring you
                down.=Yeah?
03              (silence)
...
11   N:         You're gonna have to hold me:.
12                     (0.2)
13   N:         Because I'm scared.
14                     (0.2)
15   PiC:       What?
16                     (0.2)
17   N:         You'll have to hold me.
18                     (1.0)
19   PiC:       Wait a minu[te I don't want to know all that]
20   N:                    [Because I'm the one who's       ]
21              scared of hei:ghts:.
22                     (0.3)
23   N:         Are you scared of heights?
24   N:         Obviously not. cos you're up there.
25                     (1.9)
```

At line 11, N tells PiC, "You're gonna have to hold me:.". By placing
stress on "me", N highlights the unusual order of events; making
N the person who needs the help. N goes on to give an account,
"Because I'm scared." (line 13). PiC, having been quiet so far,
shows he does not follow and says, "What?" (line 15). Saying
"what" leaves open that PiC has trouble understanding and
leaves open a possibility for N to revise their prior talk (Drew,
1997). In the next turn, N disattends PiC's attempt to repair
understanding by continuing with the project of 'being helpless'
for PiC's to step in and help. It is clear this strategy worked to
throw off PiC's expectation of what should happen at this point
(PiC is the one needing the rescue, not the other way around).
After the long 1.0 second of silence at line 18, PiC makes his
explicit his confusion: "wait wait a minute I don't want to know
all of that" (line 19). Rather than treating PiC's response as a

rejection, N continues with her plan and uses irrefutable logic (see Chapter 5) to justify why she's the one in need of PiC's help in getting her down, "because I'm the one who's scared of heights." (lines 20–21). N maintains she is afraid of heights while challenging PiC on whether he might also be afraid of heights; the logic here is "You can't be scared since you've climbed up on a roof." (not shown). On the surface, this move seems risky as these situations are volatile and can change in a moment. However, our N proceeds to push for an agreement and gets it.

```
Example 6.12: You'll have to hold me (cont'd)
26   N:      Can I do that.
27                (4.2)
28   PiC:    All right,
29                (0.2)
30   N:      Yeah?
31                (0.2)
32   PiC:    Yeah.
```

N pushes by continuing the trajectory and asking PiC, "Can I do that." (line 26), where the emphasis on "Do" is about N coming up to be with PiC, which is different to asking or directing PiC to come down. The long 4.2 seconds of silence is important here. By remaining silent without a further push of the agenda, N allows space for PiC's agreement to come off as his 'on his terms' and as his independent decision to accept that he will help N (Stokoe et al., 2020). Thus, agreeing at line 28 does not undermine PiC's autonomy to stay put for now.

We see using role-reversal as a strategy for influencing PiC without challenging their autonomy, while simultaneously demonstrating N1's commitment to the situation. N1's commitment is evident in Example 6.13. When N1 comes off as upset, and PiC is the one doing the reassuring, role reversal becomes apparent. Before the example, PiC was engaging with N1 but became unresponsive. N1 works to regain contact with PiC with a summons, which, after three rounds, is met with silence each time. In this example, we focus on how N1 regains PiC's attention and then uses role-reversal to get PiC to engage.

```
Example 6.13: Starting to get fed up
01  N1:      Kei:th,
02               (1.9)
03  N1:      Don't ignore me,
04               (1.5)
05  PiC:     I'm not ignoring ya.
06               (.)
07  N1:      Well then a:nswer me.
08               (4.5)
09  N1:      I'm starting to get a bit fed up now,
10               (2.1)
11  PiC:     hhheh heh=
12  N1:      I A:M,=
13  PiC:     =£sorry I'm sorry about
14           [that£.]
15  N1:      [Why  ] are you laughing.
16  PiC:     I'm not trying to fucking piss
17           you [off. ]
18  N1:          [W'll-] well
19           ↑why are you ↓then.
```

In line 03, N1 shifts her strategy to gain PiC attention with "Don't ignore me," which is a direct complaint about his lack of uptake. After the silence at line 04, PiC responds with a counter that rejects her complaint (thereby rejecting her characterization of his action) when he says, "I'm not ignoring ya." (line 05). Our interest is in how N1 works to leverage this response towards opening up a dialogue with a PiC who remained silent for some time. With his response to N1's complaint, PiC shows that he can hear and understand N1 and that he can speak. With a well-prefaced directive, "well then answer me" (line 07), N1 highlights the inconsistency of PiC claiming that he is not ignoring her (line 05), when he has indeed ignored her by not engaging with her summons before line 01.

Moreover, N1's turn works to solicit PiC's attention in another manner by pursuing N1's prior summons and designing her turn to make some type of acknowledgment relevant next. N1 remains silent (line 08), treating this next slot as PiC's turn space. After the long silence, N1 leverages PiC's continued non-responsiveness by making a complaint that uses an idiomatic expression, "I'm starting to get a bit fed up now" (line 09). N1 mitigates her complaint through terms such as "starting" and "bit", thereby designing this complaint as a warning, from which PiC may infer what could happen next (e.g., she might walk away). Following 2.1 seconds of silence following this threat, PiC responds with laughter (line 11). In the immediate next turn, N1 reasserts her threat through confirmation, "I A:M," (line 12), to which PiC immediately responds with an apology, "=£sorry I'm sorry about that£." (line 13). As indicated in the transcript, N1 now has PiC's attention, and she solicits an account for why PiC is laughing and not taking her seriously (lines 15–19).

Next, PiC suggests, "you can just fucking go back to the station", challenging N1 on her real commitment in the situation. The negotiator rejects PiC's challenge with "No I CA:N't." (line 21), followed by an account, and we will see how this turns out to be productive for the negotiation.

```
Example 6.13: Starting to get fed up (cont'd)
19   PiC:   Bloody- (0.2) you can just fucking go
20          back to your station.=
21   N1:    =No I CA:N't. How can I do that.
22          You know how it works, I can't do that.
23          can I. I have to sta:nd he:re, (0.4) with you.
24               (3.1)
25   N1:    But you're telling me you're not trying
26          to piss me o:ff.
```

```
27                     (7.1)
28  N1:      It feels like you are¿ It feels like you
29           just want to upset me.
30                     (3.2)
31  N1:      Will you come do:wn.
32                     (1.5)
33  N2:      Watch your step mate,
34                     (0.3)
35  N2:      Watch your step.
```

N1's account in lines 21–23 targets PiC's own knowledge and authority and power to reason, with "You know how it works," (line 22). The negotiator brings forward evidence to the contrary of what PiC has just said, specifically of her commitment to staying put, thereby treating PiC's accusations as unfair ("But you're telling me you're not trying to piss me o:ff", lines 25–26). N1 works up this argument with a linguistic technique that solicits PiC's agreement: the "can I" ties back to the statement "I can't do that." (lines 22–23) to ask for PiC's confirmation. N1 then proceeds with a complaint, "I have to sta:nd he:re, (0.4) with you." (line 23), which is also more than a complaint: it works in service of displaying the negotiator's commitment. PiC comes down a few minutes later:

```
Example 6.13: Starting to get fed up (cont'd)
38  N3:   °Is he coming,°
39  N2:   Where
40         [do you want to come,=Which way? Over] there.
40  N1:   [Yeah. Yeah. He's coming            ]
```

LESSONS LEARNED FROM EXAMPLES 6.9–6.13

- Negotiators target concerns that are in the person in crisis's domain of knowledge, giving them the advantage of control
- Negotiators identify opportunities to take risks and challenge the person in crisis.

- Role-reversal work to show negotiators' commitment to the person in crisis and can shift the person in crisis's expectations about the negotiator, and the situation.

SUMMARY

A person in crisis has, from their point of view, made a rational decision to end their life, and the negotiators do well to acknowledge these basic 'terms of agreement'. But persons in crisis rarely if ever agree to come down. This chapter has provided an overview of the interactional circumstances, co-constructed by negotiators, in which PiCs *decide* to come down, without agreeing to it.

TAKE AWAY PRACTICAL STRATEGIES: HOW TO SCAFFOLD A PERSON IN CRISIS'S DECISION TO 'COME DOWN'

- Although persons in crisis resist coming down, facilitate their autonomy to decide to come down
- Being pushy (repeating things) may lead to escalation or disengagement
- When negotiators foreground persons in crisis' agency and control, progress is made
- Targeting practical concerns (e.g., paths or strategies for coming down) can be productive – instead of asking the person in crisis to commit or agree to coming down, which is counter-productive
- Making moves that show irritation, or asking for help from the person in crisis, can be effective (at the right time)!

REFERENCES

Hogan, K. E., & Pressley, M. E. (1997). *Scaffolding student learning: Instructional approaches and issues*. Cambridge, MA: Brookline Books.

Humă, B., Stokoe, E., & Sikveland, R.O. (2020). Vocabularies of social influence: Managing the moral accountability of influencing another. *British Journal of Social Psychology, 60*(2), 319–339.

Ireland, C. A., & Vecchi, G. M. (2009). The Behavioral Influence Stairway Model (BISM): a framework for managing terrorist crisis situations? *Behavioral Sciences of Terrorism and Political Aggression, 1*(3), 203–218.

Kelln, B., & McMurtry, C. M. (2007). STEPS–structured tactical engagement process: a model for crisis negotiation. *Journal of Police Crisis Negotiations, 7*(2), 29–51.

McMains, M., & W. Mullins. (2014). *Crisis negotiations: Managing critical incidents and hostage situations in law enforcement and corrections.* New York: Routledge.

Miller, L. (2005). Hostage negotiation: Psychological principles and practices. *International Journal of Emergency Mental Health, 7*(4), 277–298.

Mullins, W. C. (2002). Advanced communication techniques for hostage negotiators. *Journal of Police Crisis Negotiations, 2*(1), 63–81.

Oostinga, M. S., Giebels, E., & Taylor, P. J. (2018). 'An error is feedback': The experience of communication error management in crisis negotiations. *Police Practice and Research, 19*(1), 17–30.

Stokoe, E., Humă, B., Sikveland, R. O., & Kevoe-Feldman, H. (2020). When delayed responses are productive: Being persuaded following resistance in conversation. *Journal of Pragmatics, 155,* 70–82.

Ury, W. (1991). *Getting past no: Negotiating with difficult people.* New York: Bantam Books.

Vecchi, G. M., V. B. Van Hasselt, & S.J. Romano (2005). Crisis (hostage) negotiation: Current strategies and issues in high risk conflict resolution. *Aggression and Violent Behavior, 10,* 533–551.

Backstage/ frontstage and the negotiation team

Chapter 7

DOI: 10.4324/9780429354892-7

WHAT IS THIS CHAPTER ABOUT?

As discussed in Chapter 1, crisis communication negotiators work in small teams. The team members, usually between four and six, rotate through roles as the negotiation unfolds. The primary negotiator's role is to talk directly to the person in crisis, whereas a secondary negotiator works 'behind the scenes,' supporting the ongoing negotiation. Other members lead, coordinate, and relay intelligence about the person in crisis and additional information to the team. So far, we have focused on the primary negotiator. In this chapter, we focus mainly on what the secondary negotiator does. We examine how the secondary negotiator attempts to support the primary negotiator and discover what forms of support are helpful and not. The chapter highlights the importance of closely attending to interaction features when training negotiators to work better as a team.

We ask:

How do members of the negotiation team, particularly the secondary negotiator (N2), provide effective support to the primary negotiator (N1) in their conversations with a person in crisis?

WHY IS THIS AN IMPORTANT TOPIC?

Within the limited body of research on actual, live negotiation, there is even less focus on what McMains and Mullins (2014, p. 85) describe as "the most important role on the negotiation team" – the secondary negotiator. A vital interest for us is in what the secondary negotiators reveal about their ability to analyse ongoing interaction, the live, turn-by-turn conversation between primary and person in crisis, by making suggestions that are sensible and effective, or misjudged and ineffective. The secondary negotiator is often positioned in close physical proximity to the primary to enable direct communication. However, their conversations are generally inaudible to the person in crisis (and invisible, if negotiation takes place by telephone), as the secondary negotiator remains in the 'backstage'. Our interest is in how and when the secondary negotiator takes a 'turn' in the unfolding negotiation, while not disrupting the primary negotiator's interaction with the person in crisis. We focus on whether the secondary negotiator, a third party, can analyse someone else's interaction (i.e., the primary negotiator and the person in crisis), such that they evaluate a conversational moment as requiring their input in the form of encouragement, or change of action, delivery, or strategy.

WHAT CURRENT TRAINING TELLS US ABOUT THE ROLE OF THE SECONDARY NEGOTIATOR

Across the wealth of hostage and crisis negotiation literature, the secondary negotiator is mentioned frequently. Still, there is little explicit research on or guidance for them. McMains and Mullins (2014, p. 118) note an "insufficient focus on or use of secondary negotiator". Typically, the role of the secondary negotiator is mentioned only in passing descriptions of the overall team. For example, the secondary negotiator "listens to negotiations; gathers intelligence" (Greenstone, Kosson, & Gacono, 2000, p. 391) and "permits the negotiator to ventilate and share some of the stress" (Schlossberg 1980, p. 115). McMains and Mullins (2014, p. 85) describe the role as a "pipeline between the negotiation team and primary", providing moral support. Relevant to the current chapter, the secondary negotiator may help the primary "develop verbal tactics" (ibid., p. 85) and "monitors the verbal interactions between hostage-taker and primary negotiator … [but] does not speak directly to the subject" (Greenstone et al., 2000, p. 397). The secondary negotiator, then, has an assisting role in the primary negotiator's interaction with the person in crisis but is one step removed.

In crisis negotiations, the secondary negotiator's role is to stay firmly 'backstage'. However, as we will see, regardless of whether crisis negotiations take place on the telephone or face-to-face (usually still at some distance from the person in crisis), the 'backstage' is collaboratively produced by all parties, including the person in crisis.

So, what kind of interventions do the secondary negotiators make? When do they make them sequentially? How does their entry into the negotiation display their ongoing analysis of the primary negotiator's interaction with the person in crisis? By what linguistic means do they do so? By analysing the position, turn design, and action of the secondary negotiator's suggested actions, and the primary negotiator's implementations (or not) of

Backstage/frontstage

those actions, we consider the secondary negotiator's ongoing negotiation analysis and the effectiveness of their interventions. In so doing, we offer perhaps the first demonstration of how secondary negotiators give advice to primary negotiators.

For instance, we show how support is enacted through praise or encouragement, and through suggestions of what to say and how to say it. We also examine if and how the primary negotiator incorporates them into the negotiation and what happens next. While some suggestions are useful, others disrupt the flow of the negotiation and the relationship between the primary negotiator and person in crisis.

TWO CORE WAYS THROUGH WHICH SECONDARY NEGOTIATORS ENACT THEIR ROLE

As we showed in Chapter 1, the core interests of conversation analysts, and core mechanics of social interaction, come to life in crisis negotiation. In crisis negotiation, if a secondary negotiator is to participate in the ongoing interaction between two other parties, and remain backstage to that encounter, then they must engage in a live conversation analysis. The secondary negotiators must identify actions and the words participants used to embody that action. They must identify what type of action came before and what might happen next, and so on, such that they may be able to insert a turn that does not disrupt the finely-calibrated and millisecond-by-millisecond timing of interaction. This requires deciding, from tacit evaluation of the ongoing interaction, that something other than its current composition of turns and actions may bring about a closer alignment between negotiator and person in crisis.

We begin by describing two interactional environments in which secondary negotiators participate in ongoing negotiations. First, in Example 7.1, we show that secondary negotiators produce an answer to the person in crisis, to be animated by the primary negotiator with the person in crisis as a recipient. Example 7.1 comes from the early stages of negotiation. PiC is located on top of a building near his own home. The negotiators are located on the ground next to the building, such that PiC can see both primary (N1) and secondary (N2) negotiator, and he occasionally hides from the negotiators' view behind the branches next to the building. The primary negotiator's focus is to get PiC to put down a knife he is holding and fulfil an earlier commitment to "come down in fifteen minutes". We join the negotiation as a changeover between negotiation team members occurs. A new secondary negotiator (speaking below) replaces the previous one.

```
Example 7.1: Who's he
01   PiC:    Who's he,
02                   (1.9)
03   N2:     °°I'm with the police, just tell him.°°
04                   (0.4)
05   N1:     He's with the police Patrick,
```

Example 7.1 illustrates what happens when PiC topicalizes N2's presence or makes his queries or challenges relevant. Also, notice how parties simultaneously (re)establish a participation framework with the secondary negotiator backstage. How does this happen?

At line 01, PiC has noticed that a new negotiator is entering the scene and asks, "Who's he", selecting N1 as the next speaker. He does not ask N2, "Who are you?". N2 maintains his backstage participation by directing his reply to N1 at low volume, designed only for the N1 to hear. He produces a response for N1 to articulate. N2's turn contains an imperative "just tell him", which is one practice for framing the words to be animated by the primary negotiator. However, some reformulation is required; N2 does not intend N1 to do a direct repeat. N2 uses the pronoun "I" not "he", creating complex issues of recipiency. While the entire turn is designed exclusively for N1, and "I am ... just tell him" are directed solely at N1, only "with the police" is designed for PiC as the recipient.

Note that N2's turn is located after a long gap develops at line 02, during which N1 has not responded to PiC's question. The gap affords interactional space for N2 to speak without overlap. More importantly, it reveals his ongoing analysis of the sequence launched by PiC at line 01, including the completeness of the turn and TCU and its action. PiC answers with a question

("Who's he"). "Who" may be the name of N2 or his role; we found that negotiators formulate "who they are" both ways. N2's turn at line 03 reveals his tacit analysis both of line 01 and line 02, including that 1.9 is a gap sufficiently long to reveal trouble in responding and the kind of response that would be apposite. At line 05, N1 produces N2's suggested answer but replaces their 'I' pronoun with 'he': "He's with the police Patrick,". In so doing, all three parties maintain the backstage participation framework and N1 and PiC as interlocutors.

In contrast to Example 7.1, Example 7.2 shows N2 offering support or endorsement of N1 with turns designed only for N1 – but, given their function, ultimately also for the person in crisis. It comes from the same negotiation, a few seconds later. N1 is trying to get PiC to put down a knife. PiC has, five minutes previously, promised to come down in 15 minutes.

```
Example 7.2: Keep going
01  N1:     Remember what you said. (.) You said
02          fifteen minutes,
03              (1.5)
04  N1:     You've got the knife in your ha:nd now?
05              (0.7)
06  PiC:    It hasn't been fifteen minutes.
07  N1:     No. Of course it hasn't. No.
08              (1.0)
09  N1:     But you can put the knife do:wn¿
10              (1.4)
11  N1:     Nothing to worry about,
12              (2.5)
13  N2:     °°°Keep- keep going°°°
14              (3.0)
15  N1:     Patrick?
16              (.)
17  PiC:    Yeah,
18              (1.2)
19  N1:     It's much nicer when I can see='at's it¿
```

While Example 7.1 illustrates how N2 may supply candidate answers to a person in crisis's question, his intervention in Example 7.2 appears in a different sequential environment. Our focus is on N2's turn at line 13, which, like "tell him" in Example 1, has an imperative-formatted design: "°°°Keep- keep going°°°". It is produced at low volume, for only N1 to hear. However, before we see what happens next, it may not be clear whether N2 is instructing N1 to say these words to PiC, or if those words support the unfolding course of action N1 initiated.

At the start of this episode, N1 produces a declarative turn with rising intonation, for PiC to "put the knife do:wn¿" (line 09). The turn-initial "but" marks a contrast with the agreed fact (as formulated by PiC) that 15 minutes have not yet passed; nevertheless, PiC can still "put the knife down". That is, while agreeing that the timeline for PiC's own promise to come down has not yet passed, N1 proposes that putting the knife down is independent of that promise. This is not the first time N1 requested that PiC put the knife down, and N1 deals with PiC's ongoing resistance in a second turn. After a gap develops (line 10), he reassures PiC that there is "Nothing to worry about,".

In response to N2's imperative to "°°°Keep- keep going°°°", N1 produces a summons to PiC. He does not animate N2's instruction. Nor does N2 include components in his turn to 'say' or 'tell him', which would transform the action into one designed for N1 to deliver to PiC. Thus, "°°°Keep- keep going°°°" is an analysis and endorsement of the primary negotiator's current strategy of formulating turns that are aligned with PiC's stated intentions (to come down) and reassure him. Moreover, it occurs at the moment in the interaction when PiC does not outright reject N1's reasoning and thereby might be on his way to go along with his proposal. We have found that in settings in which one party is attempting to persuade their recipient to do something that they had previously outright resisted doing, the resistant party's next turns are regularly delayed (Stokoe et al., 2020). It appears that such delays locate a 'change of mind' in the recipient's domain; that is, their own decision to, say, come down, rather than agree to do so.

While N2 designs a turn that supports N1 to pursue his current trajectory, rather than do something else, N1 changes the strategy at line 15. Given that N2's turn is not part of the negotiation itself, a gap of almost six seconds has developed between the person in crisis and N1's last turn at line 11. N1's strategy is to use the person in crisis's name – "Patrick?" – which works as a summons to get an almost immediate response (line 17). Names have this function in the negotiations, to reinitiate interaction when persons in crisis stop taking turns (Sikveland, 2019). If N2 had said "Say his name" at line 14, this would likely be an effective suggestion to make. Saying, "°°°Keep- keep going°°°" does not derail the negotiation. But, as we will see later in the chapter, N2's turns can easily do so.

LESSONS LEARNED FROM EXAMPLES 7.1–7.2

- Secondary negotiators enact the provision of support through their ability to analyse the ongoing interaction between the primary negotiator and the person in crisis.
- Secondary negotiators can support the primary negotiator by endorsing the current lines of action (e.g., "keep going").
- Secondary negotiators regularly 'author' turns for the primary negotiator to 'animate' with the person in crisis as the recipient and the secondary negotiator remaining in the backstage. For a successful implementation, backstage turns are timed such that the primary negotiator can hear them and deliver them – with some reformulations of, for example, pronoun choice – without disrupting the overall pace of the negotiation and while maintaining the appearance of a one-to-one conversation with the person in crisis.

In the next section, we examine additional examples of the practice introduced in Example 7.2, where the secondary negotiator's spoken turns are designed for the primary negotiator as primary recipient, before returning to examine more instances of secondary negotiator-authored turns for the primary negotiator's animation.

IT'S NOT WHAT YOU SAY BUT THE WAY THAT YOU SAY IT

In Example 7.3, N1 has been negotiating face-to-face, albeit at a short distance, for over an hour with PiC, Jessica. PiC has been slowly asphyxiating herself by hanging. PiC's front door is open, but an additional barred grille gate is locked. There have been productive moments throughout the negotiation, and PiC has implied that she might throw the gate keys to N1. However, we join the interaction as she starts to tighten the noose, subsequently becoming unresponsive. PiC's dog is barking; the moment is filled with tension.

```
Example 7.3: Keep calm
01   N1:      Jessi[ca¿         ]
02   Dog:          [((barking))]  ((barking))
03                      (0.4)
04   N1:      >JESSICA.<
05                      (0.2)
06   Dog:     ((barking))
07                      (0.4)
08   N2:      °°Keep calm°°
09   N1:      JESSICA.
10                      (0.3)
11   N1:      Throw the keys.
12   Dog:     ((bark))
13   N1:      Do it now.
```

Our focus is on N2's turn at line 08: an imperative-formatted instruction to N1 to "°°Keep calm°°". Like in Example 7.2, it is delivered at low volume and is not accompanied by features that construct it as authored words to be animated by N1. That is, N2 is not suggesting that N1 urge PiC to "keep calm"; in this instance, it is clear who the recipient is (unlike other cases, as we will see shortly). However, N2's turn comprises advice, or instructional guidance, for the emotional stance N1 should display. In response to N2, N1 maintains but does not further intensify, the prosodic features of a third summons ('JESSICA.') (see Sikveland, 2019). Shortly after this sequence, PiC manages to throw her keys and the negotiators enter the house and rescue her.

Example 7.4 contains another example of N2 imperative-formatted advice about the emotional valence N1 might productively display. PiC is positioned on top of a building after an earlier attempted burglary and has expressed fear that the police will come and 'get him'. The negotiators are positioned outside, at the bottom of the building.

```
Example 7.4: Sound angry
01  N1:     Hello::?
02               (2.8)
03  N1:     Hello:::.
04               (1.8)
05  N1:     I'm he::re?
06               (3.3) / ((PiC speaking from a
                 distance))
07  N2:     [Janet?]
08  N1:     [Hello:]::.
09               (0.3)
10  N2:     Janet.
11               (0.4)
12  N2:     Sound angry.
13               (0.7) / ((PiC speaking from a
                 distance))
14  N2:     Sound angry.
15               (1.7)
16  N1:     Talk to me:¿
17  PiC:    Yeah. When I ask you.
```

N1 is attempting to initiate a sequence of talk with PiC: note the multiple summonses (lines 01, 03, 08) and indicate readiness to talk (line 05). None of these turns mobilize a response. N2's repetition of "Janet" at line 10, with slightly elevated intensity, suggests that N2 did not secure N1's recipiency in the first summons, which occurs in overlap with N1's summons of PiC. Once N2 has N1's attention, he delivers the imperative to "Sound angry." This is also repeated, as the gap that develops at line 13 between N1 and N2 is apparently filled with PiC's inaudible talk. At line 16, N1 instantiates N2's guidance by formulating an imperative "Talk to me:¿" for PiC as a recipient. N1's delivery is emphatic, at elevated volume, and with slightly rising turn-final intonation. Immediately PiC starts to talk. As with Example 7.3, N2's advice has been effective: following a sequence of failed summons, PiC begins to talk immediately after N1 'sounds angry'. Note that N2's intervention does not specify a particular wording or action for N1 to animate but suggests the stance her next turn should deliver. Note further that, in both Examples 7.3 and 7.4, like Example 7.2, N2's interventions occur in the gaps that emerge following initial actions that do not get uptake from PiC.

LESSONS LEARNED FROM EXAMPLES 7.3–7.4

- Secondary negotiators provide effective support to primary negotiators by monitoring how primaries interact with persons in crisis in terms of and deliver words and turns with specific intonation.

- Secondary negotiators can place their suggested modifications to the delivery of actions in the gaps that open up when persons in crisis do not respond to what the primary negotiator has initiated.

- Suggestions both to 'sound angry' *and* 'keep calm' are effective when deployed in particular sequences and around specific actions; in these cases, summons. Our analyses show that there is not a simple recommendation about what to do with a failed summons, and that both staying calm *and* sounding angry can be effective in the right situation.

Overall, Examples 7.3 and 7.4 show how N2s make interventions on the unfolding interaction by using imperative-formatted suggestions designed to modify how N1s *deliver* their turns at talk. This type of intervention is markedly different from those in which N2s formulate turns for N1 to deliver to PiC as the primary recipient.

In the next section, we examine further instances of N2-authored turns for N1 animation, this time designed for PiC as the primary recipient with a *requested action* for N1, which are more or less specific in terms of what to repeat. Again, N2s build their intervention into ongoing spates of talk, while remaining backstage.

WHAT SECONDARY NEGOTIATORS SUGGEST PRIMARY NEGOTIATORS SHOULD SAY TO PERSONS IN CRISIS

Like Example 7.2, Examples 7.5 and 7.6 show how N2s design turns with imperative components that formulate turns for N1s to animate and deliver to PiC. In Example 7.5, PiC is located on the rooftop and the negotiators communicate with him from various locations at the ground level. In this case, we have a secondary negotiator (N2) and a third negotiator (N3). Both N2 and N3 are part of the negotiation team. We join the negotiation as N1 proposes PiC moves to another location on the roof to enable him to speak to another negotiator, Tracy, with whom PiC has previously been in contact.

```
Example 7.5: Say thank you
01  N1:    Why don't you go and sit (.)
02         on another bit.
03               (3.6)
04  N1:    ↑Sit at the other end.=Where you
05         can speak to (d-) (0.2) Tracy.
06               (0.5)
07  N3:    °Y:es:::°
08  N2:    °Thank you.°
09               (1.4)
10  N2:    °Thank you.°
11               (1.2)
12  N2:    °Say to him thank you.°
13               (0.8)
14  N1:    Thank you.
15               (0.9)
16  N2:    °Good work.°
```

N1's suggestion (line 01) for PiC to sit "on another bit", is apparently met with resistance. After a long gap develops, N1 instructs PiC to "↑Sit at the other end.", adding an account ("=Where you can speak to … Tracy."). This time, PiC apparently embodies compliance, given the third negotiator's whispered assessment "°Y:es:::°" (line 07) designed for negotiators only to hear.

N1's negotiation is, then, at this point, effective. At line 08, N2 says "°Thank you.°" Given that he repeats this at line 10, and then redesigns his turn at line 12, it is clear that N2's first "°Thank you.°" was designed as a turn to be animated by N1. However, until N2 includes the imperative component "Say to him", it is not treated by N1 as such. Perhaps N1 thinks N2 appreciates his effective negotiation, or that N1 is resisting N2's suggestion, foregrounding his autonomy and agency. Using the imperative may be analysed as an instantiation of N2's entitlement to direct N1 or as an embodiment of some prior social-institutional relationship between the two. However, we also suggest that the use of brief 'say' imperatives is constrained by the limited interactional space available to intervene as a backstage third party. Quite simply, a more 'polite' direction ("Could you say thank you here?"; "Just wondering if you could say thank you") takes more time. Indeed, at line 14, N1 calls, "Thank you." to PiC, but it is several seconds *after* he has complied with N1's instruction and thereby is delayed, like an afterthought. It is unclear whether saying 'thank you' is interactionally consequential; it seems to be lost in the ether as a standalone turn. At line 16, N2 produces an appreciation of N1's work, making recipiency clear by using different words ("good work") and dispensing with a 'say' imperative.

In Example 7.5, the inclusion of "Say to him" disambiguates the action and recipient of N2's turns. In Example 7.6, N1 is trying to get PiC to talk to her, and, like N2's interventions in Examples 7.2–7.4, the suggestions are designed to modify N1's turns and mobilize responses.

```
Example 7.6: Difficult hearing him
01   N1:      Come o:n. Come and talk [to me:,
```

```
02   PiC:                                [(        )
03   N2:    Say- say you're finding it
04          diffi[cult (.) h:earing him.=
05   PiC:        [(        )
06   N2:    ='n- (0.2) you'd like to see him,
07              (0.4)
08   N1:    I can't HEAR you:::¿
09              (0.3)
10   N1:    You need to come forward so I can
11          see you and hear you bette:r.
12              (4.3)
13   N1:    Come on, I need to know that
14          you're safe up the:re.
15   N2:    °That's it,°
```

In contrast to Example 7.5, N2's say-preface appears at the start of his first suggested turn for N1 to animate, ensuring that N1 understands its intended recipient. N2's words also require some transformation in footing, from 'you' and 'him' to 'I' and 'you'. N1 animates the function of N2's turn, but not its precise design. Note her addition of accounting for the imperative-formatted request "You need to come forward *so I can see you and hear you bette:r.*" (lines 10–11). After a long gap, N1 pursues a response from PiC ("Come on."). At line 15, N2 produces a turn designed for N1 (note the whispered volume), "That's it", which is responsive not to PiC moving, but a positive assessment of N1 for having said the right sort of thing. While PiC does not "come forward" for some time, he becomes verbally engaged.

N2's suggestion is placed in a slot that is not overlapping either PiC or N1's talk. It also occurs as N1 has repeatedly requested that PiC "talks" to her. As we have seen in Chapter 3, PiCs routinely resist proposals and requests to "talk" in these negotiations, on the basis that "talk does not do anything". Whether or not this is the tacit expertise N2 displays here, his intervention is precisely timed, in terms of sequential position, and offers a change of strategy when a repeated request has failed.

In Example 7.7, N2 adds "try" to his say-prefaced turn, which reduces the constraint for N1 to formulate a *direct* repetition of whatever N2 suggests.

```
Example 7.7: I don't mean to offend you
01   PiC:    Y- you smile (.) as if: (.)
02           it's an achievement to: (1.8)
03   N1:     [Is (k-) ]
04   N2:     [°(     )] try and
05           [say look (.) I'm sorry I've tried=
06   PiC:    [to inflict: (0.5) suffering 'n
07   N2:     =to understand (what happens)°
08   N1:     I'm- I'm sorry I'm trying to
09           understand what's happening.
10                  (1.1)
11   N2:     °I don't mean to offend you.°
12   N1:     I'm not meaning to offend you.
13                  (4.3)
14   N2:     °Patrick. Please help me to understand.°
15   N1:     Patrick. Please help me to understand.
16                  (1.6)
17   N2:     °What's happened.°
18                  (0.8)
19   N1:     What's happened.
```

N2 suggests that N1 accounts (which is difficult to hear) for some earlier offence taken by PiC and apologize for it (lines 04–09). While there are subtle differences between N2's suggestions and N1's subsequent animations, N1 largely repeats N2's authored turns. He also uses similar intonation and phrasal prominence patterns as N2, who produces a 'reading' voice comprising global rise-fall across each intonation unit. Furthermore, unlike previous examples, N2 does not place his turns when there is a silence between turns, but in overlap with both N1 and PiC's ongoing turns.

LESSONS LEARNED FROM EXAMPLES 7.5–7.7

- One challenge for secondary negotiators to enact support is to be clear who the intended recipient is of any turn that they produce. Is the secondary negotiator saying something directed to the primary negotiator, or for delivery by the primary negotiator for the person in crisis?

- A practice to deal with potential ambiguity around recipiency is to include the simple word "say" before any turns produced that are intended as suggestions of things for the primary negotiator to say to persons in crisis.

- However, given that the opportunity to enact support is sometimes in only fractions of seconds, secondary negotiators also need to be as concise as possible in their suggestions.

Our analysis above shows how N2s instruct and guide N1s to animate the turns they author for PiCs as the recipient. N2s suggest sequence-closing third turns (Example 7.5) and accounts for N1's actions, including requesting turns that do not get uptake from PiCs (Examples 7.6 and 7.7). The inclusion of a say-preface to imperative suggestions clarifies intended recipiency, as shown by its inclusion after previous failed attempts to get N1 to say what N2 suggests.

The impact of secondary negotiators' suggestions varies across our three cases. In Example 7.5, N1's animation of N2's "thank you" was disconnected from its sequential fit to PiC's actions. In Example 7.6, N2's interventions appear apposite and effective, in that a positive shift in PiC's behaviour occurs almost immediately. In Example 7.7, we saw little impact of N2's interventions to mobilize a response from PiC. In the final section, we consider how secondary negotiators' interventions, particularly those targeting the person in crisis as recipient, may be fitted and apposite (or inapposite and ill-fitted) to the frontstage unfolding interaction.

HOW SECONDARY NEGOTIATORS DERAIL THE NEGOTIATION

The suggestions made by the secondary negotiator may aid ongoing negotiation but also risk derailing it either temporarily for a small number of turns or in a more sustained way, say, by initiating or escalating conflict. Example 7.8 comes from the same case as Examples 7.4 and 7.6. We join the negotiation approximately an hour into the four hours it runs overall, as N1 attempts to elicit PiC's name, something that she has pursued earlier. Some of PiC's talk across lines 05–06 and 13 is difficult to hear.

```
Example 7.8: Cos I care for you
01  N1:    What do you want me to call you.
02              (0.3)
03  PiC:   Why should I tell you my name yeah?
04  N1:    I told [you my na:me¿]
05  PiC:          [(that guy with)
06         [who was- who was there (today).
07  N2:    [°Say (it's) cos I care for you°.
08              (.)
09  PiC:   [No.  ]
10  N2:    [°Cos I] care for you°.
11              (0.2)
12  N1:    I [care for you:?]
13  PiC:     [( )(coming)  ] (down if I give) my name.
14              (0.4)
15  N1:    If I didn't care for you I wouldn't be
16         [HERE. Would I.   ]
17  PiC:   [Why do you want to] get my NAME!
18              (0.3)
19  N1:    You're not <LISTENING TO ME:>.
```

At the start of the episode, N1 does not ask PiC for his name, but what he wants her to call him. Our data show that PiCs often resist supplying their name (including surname) for many reasons, including (as in this case) following earlier criminal activity and pursuit from the police (cf. Sacks, 1992, on how callers to a Suicide

Prevention Center avoid giving their names). Given that N1 has not asked for PiC's name, one possible response to PiC's resistance is reassurance – that he does not have to give his (full) name. Instead, N1's response invokes a reciprocal obligation for mutual sociality ("I told you my na:me¿"): PiC has started talking almost as N1 responds with a largely inaudible turn.

At line 07, N2 proposes a say-prefaced account ("say (it's) cos I care for you") to PiC's objection to the original request ("Why should I tell you my name yeah?"). PiC's objection appears to get no traction. N2 repeats his suggestion, treating N1 as able to hear this as a turn to animate for PiC as the primary recipient (and not an expression of care from N2 to N1). However, it is likely that N2 repeats his suggestion because it is initially produced in overlap (lines 06–07). After a short gap in line 11, N1 animates N2's proposed account. We do not know if N1 has heard N2's suggestion both times it was produced, or whether she initially resisted animating it. In any case, although N2 authored a candidate answer to PiC's question at line 02, N1 does not produce it as an answer, but as a *new* action. By dropping the 'cos', N1 accommodates the backstage account to her interaction with PiC as the recipient.

PiC starts talking in overlap with N1's turn, extending the earlier sequence and maintaining his objection to giving his name (line 13). N1 continues to expand and account for the 'care' element she has animated, which was authored by N2: "If I didn't care for you I wouldn't be HERE. Would I." Again, however, PiC talks in overlap, reissuing and reformulating his earlier question: "Why do you want to get my NAME!" (line 17), disrupting the progressivity of the sequence. Thus, N2's suggestions have not resulted in a response that removed the need for PiC to reissue his question. It is somewhat ironic, then, that the sequence ends with N1 chastising PiC for not 'listening'.

Example 7.8 shows the potential complexities involved in crisis negotiation. When N1 and PiC are already talking in overlap, N2's interventions create problems for the encounter's progressivity. Crisis negotiation opens a double participation framework for N1 who must interact with PiC *and* N2. In the case above, N2's turns disrupt N1–PiC interaction in terms of the unfolding sequential organization and action.

Example 7.9 is structurally less complex but illustrates further inapposite interventions from N2. The case comes from the same negotiation as Example 7.3, where PiC, Jessica, is inside her house and standing on a chair with a noose around her neck. The negotiators are outside, within visible and audible range as they can see and hear PiC through a locked grille gate, to which PiC has the keys.

```
Example 7.9: What's her name
01   N1:    Tell me about the other stuff
02          that's made you feel so bad tonight.
03               (1.6)
04   PiC:   My nan (.) (was really the last
05          friend I) ~ever h:ad alive~,
06               (0.2)
07   N1:    Your what sorry?
08               (0.3)
09   PiC:   ~The LAST friend I ever H(h)AD
10          in life. that c(h)ared. (.) is dead.~
11               (0.2)
12   N1:    [Your nan.]
13   PiC:   [The last ] ~woman. That I had.~
14               (1.9)
15   N1:    And what- (0.9) were you close to your nan?
16   PiC:   HHhhh
17               (0.9)
18   PiC:   Well obviously:.
19               (2.0)
20   N2:    °°What's her name°°
21   N1:    And what- what was your nan's name,
22               (0.8)
23   PiC:   Nan.
24               (1.3)
25   N1:    You just called her nan yeah?
26   PiC:   Obviously. (She was) my nan,
```

This episode begins effectively, as PiC produces a fitted narrative response to N1's opening elicitation. We found that wh- or interrogative formatted questions containing a timeframe (line 01: 'Tell me ... so bad tonight') routinely mobilized responses from PiC, particularly after spates of conflict or resistance to talking (see Chapter 2). After a delay, PiC produces an answer to N1's question. This is an example of an effective silence to which we return in Chapter 8.

At line 07, N1 initiates repair, having not heard PiC's emotion-laden response. At line 09, PiC reformulates and slightly upgrades her response, which is produced at higher volume, with extreme case formulations, increased breathiness, and 'wobbly voice' (Hepburn 2004). N1 initiates repair again (line 12), in overlap with PiC, who produces a second partial repeat of her initial response (line 13). After a long gap, N1 asks a question that Jessica treats as inapposite. Having disclosed the loss of her nan, the "last friend" she "ever had in life", N1 asks whether PiC was "close" to her grandmother. PiC's response confirms that she was close to her nan while challenging the question's askability: "Well obviously:." (line 18).

At line 19, another long gap develops, after which N2 supplies a turn for N1 to animate. The selection of this location reveals N2's ongoing analysis of the emerging disfluency and misalignment in the sequence after a promising start. In this case, N2 does not use a say-preface or other turn design features but simply whispers "°°What's her name°°" (line 20). N1 immediately animates the action directed at PiC, replacing "her" with "your nan" and initiating the turn with an and-preface to connect it to N1-PiC prior talk. After a delay, PiC responds. The delay and delivery indicate further emerging disaffiliation between PiC and N1; after another delay, N1 asks a question that PiC treats as having an already-known answer, and thus inapposite (cf. Stokoe & Edwards, 2008, on 'silly questions'): "You just called her nan ... Obviously she was my nan".

LESSONS LEARNED FROM EXAMPLES 7.8–7.9

- Both examples show how secondary negotiators may negatively impact the ongoing negotiation by making inapposite suggestions for the primary negotiator to say to the person in crisis.

- In Example 7.8, reassuring PiC that they do not need their name, just something to call them, might be better suited to the unfolding sequence than "I care for you", which seems oriented to the relationship between N1 and PiC, but is easy to resist.
- In Example 7.9, suggesting that N1 opens up more opportunities for PiC to talk about her grandmother may more effectively scaffold what PiC wants to talk about than expanding on N1's unproductive question, "were you close".

The final section has described instances in which the secondary negotiator interventions disrupt the negotiation's progressivity or are misaligned with the person in crisis's turns. When compared to interventions for which N1 is the primary recipient, it appears that suggesting candidate turns for N1 to animate is a riskier practice. We consider our accumulated findings in the next section.

SUMMARY

This chapter has lent empirical scrutiny to how secondary negotiators actually enact 'support' in the negotiation team. Discovering what works and what is less effective in such

---

TAKEAWAY PRACTICAL STRATEGIES: WHAT CAN SECONDARY NEGOTIATORS DO?

- To ensure that the primary negotiator knows who your intended recipient is, try adding "say" to the start of any turns that you want them to deliver to the person in crisis.
- Effective support often comes in the form of recommendations of *how* to say things, through modifying intonation rather than *what* to say.
- To make an effective recommendation of what to say, avoid suggesting generic 'rapport-building' tactics such as "I care for you!". Instead, ensure that suggestions are fitted precisely to the current position of the person in crisis.

---

encounters helps negotiators to understand their practice, with the goal for stressful encounters to nevertheless progress as smoothly as they can ever be. On this basis, it seems safe to recommend to secondary negotiators that they make fewer suggestions grounded in the classic tropes of 'rapport' and more on what the evidence from real negotiations shows is effective.

REFERENCES

Greenstone, J. L., Kosson, D. S., & Gacono, C. B. (2000). Psychopathy and hostage negotiations: Some preliminary thoughts and findings. In Gacono, C.B (Ed.), *The clinical and forensic assessment of psychopathy* (pp. 385–404). London: Routledge.

Hepburn, A. (2004). Crying: Notes on description, transcription, and interaction. *Research on Language and Social Interaction, 37*(3), 251–290.

McMains, M., & W. Mullins. (2014). *Crisis negotiations: Managing critical incidents and hostage situations in law enforcement and corrections.* New York: Routledge.

Sacks, H. (1992). *Lectures on conversation,* Vols I and II, edited by Gail Jefferson. Oxford: Blackwell.

Schlossberg, H. (1980). Values and organization in hostage and crisis negotiation teams. *Annals of the New York Academy of Sciences, 347*(1), 113–116.

Sikveland, R. O. (2019). Failed summons: Phonetic features of persistence and intensification in crisis negotiation. *Journal of Pragmatics, 150,* 167–179.

Stokoe, E., & Edwards, D. (2008). 'Did you have permission to smash your neighbour's door?' Silly questions and their answers in police-suspect interrogations. *Discourse Studies, 10*(1), 89–111.

Stokoe, E., Humă, B., Sikveland, R. O., & Kevoe-Feldman, H. (2020). When delayed responses are productive: Being persuaded following resistance in conversation. *Journal of Pragmatics, 155,* 70–82.

From practice to training
Chapter 8

WHAT IS THIS CHAPTER ABOUT?

Throughout this book, we have shown how crisis professionals handle the interactional opportunities and challenges that occur from the early stages of the crisis through to their successful resolution. In negotiations with suicidal individuals, successful resolution occurs when the person in crisis moves to safety and thus enacts a decision to choose life. We have identified the communicative practices that comprise negotiators' expertise and skills, and why these skills are essential to crisis negotiations. We have placed a series of aspects of negotiation practice under the microscope, guiding readers through the conversation analytic science that underpins the training tips

DOI: 10.4324/9780429354892-8

provided throughout. Now it is time to step back from the detailed analyses to consider more broadly how the conversation analysis of crisis talk can inform training for negotiators and other professionals dealing with people in conflict and crisis.

The chapter is structured around three themes emerging from our research findings, all key to successful crisis negotiations. The three themes are:

1. Making questions work: Question formats and effective silences.
2. Choosing the right words: What it really means to build rapport.
3. Scaffolding a resolution: How to support their agenda, not our own.

We consider these themes based on an overall interpretation of our findings. While it is beyond the remit of our research to evaluate the relevance of existing recommendations or training models, we propose how our research can inform, and be informed by, some established training concepts, especially those cited under the umbrella term 'Active Listening Skills' (ALS).

We ask:

What are the implications of our research on negotiator practice for negotiator training?

WHY IS THIS AN IMPORTANT TOPIC?

Professionals learn tacitly by doing their job and by reflecting upon the trial and error of practice. However, an important foundation for learning takes place in training. We undoubtedly see this with hostage and crisis negotiators. Our research bridges training and practice by maximizing the symmetry between what negotiators get trained to do and what they actually do in real-life situations.

Through many years of experience in turning conversation analytic research into training, we have found that when people are asked to report on, *post-hoc*, what they say they do may be completely different from what they actually do (Stokoe, 2014; Sikveland & Stokoe, 2017). They may report what they *think* they do (but do not), or report what they ought to do (but do not). Either way, we argue that negotiation training should be based on evidence of what negotiators do on the job – the tacit experience and expertise that they have when the stakes are genuinely life or death – thereby securing a cohesive link between rhetoric of professional guidelines and the reality of doing negotiation.

WHAT DOES CURRENT TRAINING TELL US?

The concept of Active Listening Skills (ALS), as incorporated in the Behavioural Influence Stairway Model (BISM) (e.g., Vecchi, Van Hasselt, & Romano, 2005; Ireland & Vecchi, 2009), is intuitively well-placed and relevant to negotiation.

The active listening skills are:

- Open questions
- Effective silences
- Emotional labelling
- Minimal encouragers (e.g., "mm", nodding)
- Mirroring (e.g., repetition of what the interlocutor has just said)
- Paraphrasing (rephrasing the interlocutor's statement in your own words)
- "I"-messages (e.g., "I feel X when you Y, because Z")
                    (see e.g., Miller, 2005, for an overview)

Active listening is based on the understanding that a negotiator cannot force change but needs to achieve positive change through listening and reacting to what the recipient has to say. Thus, training recommends using 'soft' tactics instead of 'hard' ones to lay the foundations to overcome resistance and influence the person as the negotiation proceeds (Ireland & Vecchi, 2009). It is argued that 'soft' tactics make it hard for a person in crisis to say 'no.' In other words, 'go slow to go fast' (Ury, 1991, as presented in Mullins, 2002).

If negotiators are advised to use ALS and 'soft' tactics, it follows that amongst the features to *avoid* are:

- Being confrontational
- Arguing and yelling
- Moralizing (e.g., "what kind of person does something like this?")
- Diagnosing
- Using the wrong names

At an overarching level, a slow, stepwise process is also evident in our research. And at a more granular level, we have shown how effective listening happens turn-by-turn (Sikveland, Kevoe-Feldman, & Stokoe, 2020; Stokoe & Sikveland, 2020). There is no simple way of reducing these listening skills to a set of words or phrases that will do the job. Effective listening requires moment-by-moment accommodation. *A priori* factors and variables may be less useful to negotiators than understanding what actually works in terms of words to say and turns to take (Sikveland et al., 2020).

For these reasons, we need to exercise caution when recommending more specific strategies for a successful negotiation. Appreciations ("thank you"), positive evaluations and compliments ("you're doing really well"), and labelling emotions ("you sound angry") may be recommended at the early stages of negotiations (see e.g., Miller, 2005), but using them effectively requires caution and experience. We provide evidence for *how* and *what* may constitute the relevant contexts for specific ALS strategies and what such 'experience' may look like in the interaction, based on what negotiators do in real-life situations.

In our data, cases representative of 'emotional labelling', 'mirroring', 'paraphrasing', and '"I"-messages' actually occur infrequently and thus are hard to assess. In contrast, questions and silences are frequent and key to the negotiators' conduct and success. But what types of questions and silences are these? And what makes questions and silences work effectively? As we summarize each of the three themes emerging from our research, we highlight how to recognize when our research helps specify contexts in which known ALS strategies work well, and circumstances where they do not work as well.

MAKING QUESTIONS WORK: QUESTION FORMATS AND EFFECTIVE SILENCES

Asking questions is key to moving the negotiation forwards. Designing an effective question means having a finely tuned question format and knowing the type of constraint it places on the recipient. For example, it is incorrect to assume that yes/no questions are 'closed' and that they generate only one-word responses. generate one-word answers. They can be designed to elicit one-word answers, but it is common that people say more words in response. It is also not the case that all wh-questions or "Tell me about X" questions are 'open' and more productive in negotiations than yes/no questions. Indeed, we find that negotiators use yes/no questions to drive the conversation forward in a non-coercive manner. The reason is grounded in conversation analytic findings that show how, for participants, yes/no questions make relevant more than simply a "yes" or "no" response. Responses to such questions typically get an elaboration (with or without a confirming "yes"), or "no" + account for why.

A yes/no question can take a conversation in positive new directions and Example 8.1 illuminates this point. We join the negotiation 90 minutes after its start. The person in crisis (PiC) has previously been involved with social services but now, since he has turned 18 years old, he is no longer eligible for their support. He is concerned that his situation will worsen by agreeing to come to the police station and has explicitly rejected the negotiator's (N's) proposals that it would be helpful for PiC. Our target question occurs in line 01: "Have you heard of Mind at all?", which is a yes/no-formatted question.

```
Example 8.1: Have you heard of Mind
01   N:      Have you heard of Mi:nd at all?
02                   (1.9)
03   PiC:    Say that again,
04   N:      Have you heard of Mi:nd,
05                   (3.0)
06   PiC:    I've seen a poster on the bus,
```

We noticed that, in stark contrast to the conversation up to this point in the negotiation, in which PiC has rejected N's various proposals, PiC now responds with something that opens the possibility of more talk. Included in N's design of the question is asking about a mental health charity called "Mind." By asking whether PiC has heard of the charity, N offers PiC an alternative to the police - which might be more inviting. The question ends with "at all", reducing the assumption that PiC ought to have heard about "Mind". Rather than immediately rejecting N's question, PiC delays an immediate response with silence (line 02), then asks N to repeat the question (line 03). N repeats the question (line 04), and then after another delay at line 05, PiC confirms knowledge about "Mind" from a bus poster (line 06). PiC's response shows that he knows about "Mind" and opens for the possibility that he as some knowledge about the organization, or is willing to learn more about it. With his response, PiC aligns with N's course of action, which serves as a starting point for N to propose a solution to the crisis. Example 8.1 shows how questions other than typical wh- and "tell me..."-formats are productive for moving the conversation forwards while maintaining PiC's rights to agency and control.

The effectiveness of asking questions is in not just how they are asked but also how they are followed up in the next turn. Example 8.2 is another example of how yes/no questions are usually responded to with something more than a single "yes" or a "no". In this example, the person in crisis (PiC) calls an emergency line while sitting on the edge of a bridge threatening to jump. In an attempt to move them to safety, the dispatcher (DIS) asks a yes/no question (line 139), then makes productive use of PiC's "yeah". In effect, PiC agrees that it would be safer to move away from the ledge.

```
Example 8.2: Off the bridge
135 DIS:    But yih know
136         when yer mind switches t'wanting t' jump
137         again you shouldn't be nea:r it.
138             (.)
139 DIS:    Yih kno:w. Don't you think that would help?
```

```
140  PiC:    Yea:h.
141  DIS:    So: how 'bout you jus' get offa tha:t¿
142                 (0.2)
143  PiC:    What about if I cli:mb over:. on thee
144          other side of th' sidewa:lk.
```

In lines 135–137, DIS expresses concern that, whilst being
so close to the edge, PiC might more easily decide he cannot
change, spontaneously jump, or that an accident might happen.
In line 139, the question, "Don't you think that would help?"
points back at a proposal to move away from the edge. PiC
answers, "Yea:h." (line 140), thus agreeing that moving away
from the edge is a good idea. DIS pursues this logic in line 141,
"So: how 'bout you jus' get offa tha:t¿", to which PiC proposes
to climb over to the other side of the sidewalk (lines 143–144).
We see here that a simple yes/no question works to get a PiC
to move to safety. At no point does PiC explicitly *agree* to move:
the proposal in lines 143–144 is designed to show moving is *his*
decision, and that he retains the autonomy to make up *his own*
mind, by initiating *his own* actions.

People ask questions to reduce the gap between what they
know and what they do not know. But asking questions has
a purpose beyond information gathering: with questions we
get to know each other and the world around us. Indeed, our
research suggests that asking questions is the most effective
way to build relationships and show commitment to a person in
crisis.

Examples 8.3 and 8.4 offer side-by-side comparisons of
what happens when N tries to engage PiC in talk by showing
appreciation for PiC, an evaluative approach for giving PiC
a reason to talk. While N attempts to get PiC to talk about
something only he knows (lines 03–06), this method fails to
engage PiC productively. PiC is barricaded in his flat, and N
repeatedly phones him, attempting to start a conversation. PiC
keeps hanging up.

```
Example 8.3:  It's important to you it's important
              to me
01            ((ring))
02  PiC:      Hello?
03  N:        .ptk hello Kevin=it's Steve.
04            Thanks for: uh >putting your
05            phone< back on,.hhh uh: I'd ↑like
06            to talk to you a bit more about this
07            pee cee North.=cos it's obviously-
08            it's- I mean it's something that's
09            very important to you.=It's
10            important to me:.
11                 (.)
12  N:        To find out what's going on.
13                 (0.2)
14  N:        .hhh
15  PiC:      ((hangs up))
```

After PiC picks up the phone (02), N introduces himself and greets PiC before displaying appreciation that PiC is willing to talk to him, "Thanks for: uh >putting your phone< back on," (lines 04–05). Not expecting any response (N continues talking), N presents his purpose of calling: "I'd like to talk to you a bit more about this pee cee North." (lines 05–07). PC North is, according to PiC, a member of the police who had treated him unfairly earlier that day in connection with an injunction. N is here displaying an interest in knowing more about the situation and also providing an account as he continues in lines 08–10: "it's something that's very important to you.=It's important to me:.". Here, N is not using a question but instead presents a purpose and account for mutual benefit. It turns out that PiC has no interest in providing further details at this point, and he hangs up in line 15.

In this negotiation case, the negotiators keep calling PiC, each time changing their linguistic approach. In the next attempt (Example 8.4), N succeeds in getting PiC to talk by asking a "can you tell me..."-framed question (line 04).

```
Example 8.4: I can do something about it
01   PiC:   Ye=hello:.
02   N:     Hello Kevin=it's Steve.
03          (1.0)
04   N:     .hh Kevin- (.) can you tell me:
05          a bit more about pee cee North
06          so I can do something about it.
07   PiC:   Ri:ght. (0.3) six months ago: (0.2) there
08          was a::- Big Power had a call injunction
09          to come in the house ((continues))
```

In this example, the "Can you tell me" (line 04) part of the question might appear as a yes/no format, and therefore closed-ended. However, the use of the verb form "can" transforms the action of the question into a request that elicits PiC's point of view, focusing on what can be done for PiC ("so I can do something about it."), rather than merely talking things through. PiC immediately answers and provides details about what had happened earlier in the day. Comparing these two attempts (Examples 8.3 and 8.4), we can see how questions are effective for engaging PiC, whereas not asking (instead) is ineffective. In Example 8.3, N accounts for his purpose in terms of his own and PiC's point of view. Persons in crisis are unlikely to affiliate with negotiators' point of view, and the negotiator has no right to assume the person in crisis's point of view. Asking a question, on the other hand, avoids assuming purpose or knowledge and lets the person in crisis speak (or not) from their domain of knowledge without the pressures of agreeing to anything the negotiator proposes. Examples 8.3–8.4 highlight our overall findings whereby appreciations and valuations of a person in crisis's conduct are not enough to get the conversation going. Negotiators need questions to engage the person in crisis and know how to use them productively.

Also key to making questions work is to allow for silences to emerge. In the training literature, these are referred to as *effective silences* (e.g., Miller, 2005). In our research, we show how and when silences are indeed effective. We find that silences and timing are effective, even crucial, in the early stages of the negotiations where negotiators pursue open-ended questions like "what happened (today)". In general, such PiC-centred questions work well to get the conversation started in crisis negotiations. We illustrate this point in Example 8.5. Here, PiC is barricaded inside her flat and threatening to take her own life (she has a noose tied to her neck).

```
Example 8.5: What's made it really bad tonight
01  PiC:   You can't save me.
02                (0.9)
03  N:     What's made it- (.) what's made it
04         really bad tonight though Jessica.=What's
05  made   i[t- what's made it [so bad. ]
06  PiC:    [Just e-          [just eve ] rythi:ng.
07  PiC:   Just everything.=(n) you know, just- just-
08         just -just- just it all.
09              (2.2)
10  PiC:   Ju[st- just- ] just- just it all.
11  N:       [Like what.]
12              (0.2)
13  N:     Like what.
14              (0.3)
15  PiC:   Just
16              (4.7)
17  PiC:   Just- just
18              (3.5)
```

In line 01 PiC presents a strong form of resistance towards the negotiation and commitment towards her decision to end life, "You can't save me.". Instead of arguing with PiC's point of view, N asks a question in PiC's domain of knowledge: "what's made it really bad tonight though Jessica." (lines 03–04). In response, and in partial overlap with N's repetition of his question in lines 04–05 ("What's made it– what's made it so bad."), PiC answers "just everythi:ng." (line 06). What is especially worth noting so far in this sequence is that N acknowledges that something is indeed "really bad" and warranting PiC's strong upset, while also opening for the possibility that this upset is tied to a particular point in time ("What's made it really bad <u>tonight</u>"); that is, that PiC is not necessarily or at all times feeling like this. N manages to ask a question without challenging PiC's agency or control.

Since PiC's answer, "just everythi:ng." (line 06), does not offer particular feelings or events, N pursues a specification with "like what" (line 13), and eventually PiC answers:

Example 8.5: What's made it really bad tonight (cont'd)

```
19   N:     So we- we know- (.) we know can deal with
20          the whole James thing.
21              (0.3)
22   N:     That's fine. That- that'll be easy to
23          deal with.
24              (0.3)
25   N:     Tell me about the other stuff then.
26              (1.1)
27   N:     Tell me about the other stuff that's
28          made you feel so bad tonight.
29              (1.6)
30   PiC:   My nan (.) ~(was really) the last friend
31          I ever h:ad alive~,
```

Before providing a full answer, PiC shows that she is trying: "Just" (line 15), "Just- just" (line 17) opens up a turn which N allows to proceed, initially without interfering, then, in line 19 N removes the topic of "James" (an individual who has been causing pain for PiC over some time), and asks PiC to specify beyond this topic ("tell me about the other stuff then.", line 25). Eventually, PiC opens up about her grandmother ("my nan", line 30–31), as "~the last friend I ever h:ad alive~" (~ represents crying voice). This is a golden opportunity for N to learn more, and to affiliate with PiC.

Example 8.5 thus shows an example of how wh-questions like "what happened (today)" can work to facilitate talk and relationship building. The key here is to allow for silences to emerge: the silences are crucial for PiC to start answering and giving her time to show deliberation as she prepares to answer the question.

How do negotiators know how long to wait? Our research shows this is best treated as an open-ended question, to which there is no clear, quantitative answer. Part of being an effective negotiator is to test the potential of an effective silence, and successful negotiators accommodate their behaviours moment by moment. Consider Example 8.6, where N targets practical knowledge about how PiC made it up on the loft where he is currently located.

```
Example 8.6: I used to climb up her when I was
             little
01   N:      How- how would you- how did you
02           get up here.='n how- how
03           will you (k-)(.) sort of get
04           down from here.
05                 (2.3)
06   N:      [Did-  ]
07   PiC:    [I used] to climb up here when I was
             little.
```

In lines 01–04, N asks two questions, both related to how PiC imagines he can to move to safety. After a long delay (line 05), N and PiC begin to talk at the same time (lines 06 and 07), but N drops out of the overlapping talk ("Did–", line 06), whereas PiC proceeds to answer N's question: an informing that serves as an explanation of how he might have climbed on the roof ("I used to climb up here when I was little."). Though N cannot know that the answer will come, at this time, he accommodates by yielding the floor to PiC.

Monitoring and adjusting behaviours moment by moment is key to any conversation going smoothly and essential for negotiations to progress. We have shown how silences can be a clear indication to a negotiator that PiC is moving from strong resistance to weaker forms of resistance (Stokoe et al., 2020).

However, not all extended silences are effective. Consider Example 8.7, in which the negotiator has offered "help" which the person in crisis has resisted.

```
Example 8.7: How CAN we help you
01   N:    That's exactly why I'm here.
02         Just to see if we can help,
03                  (1.6)
04   N:    But how can we help you Oliver,
05                  (5.2)
06         ((negotiator opens up a new line of
           enquiry))
```

Here we see how the negotiator (N) formulates their entire purpose in terms of help: "That's exactly why I'm here. Just to see if we can help," (line 01). Following a 1.6 second gap (line 03), the negotiator pursues a response from PiC with the question: "But how can we help you Oliver," (line 04). With this question N targets the HOW of "help", appealing to PiC's point of view. But the question is met with extended silence (line 05) and does not lead to any uptake from PiC in the ensuing interaction. It is difficult for negotiators to pursue "help" as a relevant activity for persons in crisis to engage in. In other words, asking questions in an open-ended kind of way does not in and of itself make conversations more effective. It depends on what the negotiator is asking of the person in crisis.

FROM PRACTICE TO TRAINING: HOW NEGOTIATORS MAKE QUESTIONS WORK

1. *Yes/no questions*: While typically defined as 'closed-ended' rather than 'open-ended', negotiators regularly use yes/no questions to productively engage a person in crisis in talk about a potential solution to a problem (see Examples 8.1 and 8.2), or to get a conversation going (see Example 8.4, compared to 8.3).

2. *Open-ended questions:* Questions like, "what happened (today)?" are productive in getting the conversation started. Using these questions represents a shift away from the insistence that negotiators are there to help, to concrete ways of *how* a negotiator can help a person in crisis. Unlike statements and positive formulations of purpose ("I'm here to help"; "it's important to me/you that you tell us more"), questions are more likely to get a positive uptake from a person in crisis.

3. *Silences*: Allowing silence after a question extends the person in crisis's space and time to show they are deliberating before answering. Negotiators show tacit knowledge that some silences signal a shift from the earlier stronger forms of resistance from the person in crisis to weaker forms of resistance (Stokoe et al., 2020).

4. *Varying question format*: It is important not to rely on just one type of question format, as different questions have different uses and advantages. Negotiators modify question formats as part of their professional practice.

Further reading in this book

To learn more about how asking questions is an effective strategy for getting the conversation started, we refer to Chapter 2; methods for managing strong emotions are outlined in Chapter 4; productively challenging a person in crisis and listening to silences following strong resistance is examined in Chapter 5, and learning how to scaffold a person in crisis's decision to choose life over harm is described in Chapter 6.

CHOOSING THE RIGHT WORDS: WHAT IT REALLY MEANS TO BUILD RAPPORT

Negotiations take time and require patience. From the outset of an encounter, negotiators face strong resistance from persons in crisis. We show how such resistance is both a challenge and an opportunity for negotiators. Existing training argues that relationship building is essential to influence behaviour change in high stakes negotiations and that such relationship building is based on active listening, empathy, and rapport (Van Hasselt, Romano, & Vecchi, 2008). Establishing rapport and showing empathy by putting yourself in another's place are key tactics for relationship building (Ireland & Vecchi, 2009), and it seems that rapport occurs when people are perceived as genuine and having the right intentions. However, what such things as rapport actually look like are generally underspecified. We argue that negotiators must convey integrity, appear genuine, and express the right intentions in the midst of a tense encounter. When a person in crisis builds a wall of continued resistance, what methods can a negotiator use to show empathy? Is there a right word or phrase to convince a person in crisis to choose life? We have shown that negotiator authenticity is build turn-by-turn and moment-to-moment.

There is an ongoing risk in negotiations with a person in crisis that a negotiator may *claim* they are genuine rather than *showing* it. If the negotiator has to say, "I'm being genuine", then a person in crisis can easily challenge that claim. Creating a false sense of care appears insincere and could backfire by giving the person in crisis an additional reason to resist the negotiation. Example 8.8 shows how 'appearing genuine' can indeed backfire:

```
Example 8.8: Everyone is worried
01   N:      =I- I wanted t- I sort of like want
02           to try and get to the
03           bottom of this.=An:.hhh
04           everyone out here is sort of
05           like really worried about ya.
06                (0.4)
```

```
07   PiC:    Yeah I do you know what- I- (0.7)
08           don't [worry.  ]
09   N:            [I- I am-] I am worried:.
10   N:      <I'm r- I a:m really worried.=
11               (0.9)
12   PiC:    #°All right, Thanks°#.
13               (1.9)/ ((PiC hangs up))
14   N:      Henry.
```

Here N has phoned PiC, who is barricaded inside his flat,
threatening to end his life with a gun. N displays her intentions
in line 01, "I sort of like want to try and get to the bottom of
this." (lines 01–03), referring to PiC's situation. Then, N makes
explicit that not only her but all the co-present professionals'
intentions are genuine: "everyone out here is sort of like really
worried about ya." (lines 04–05). We may question N's use of
the modifier "sort of" here, as it may downgrade how genuine
she is. PiC does not directly question or challenge N's intentions
but disengages with it and treats it as irrelevant in lines 07–08
("Yeah I do you know what– I– (0.7) don't worry".). In answer to
this dismissal, N upgrades the genuine nature of her intentions:
first, "I am worried:" (stressing "AM", line 07), then "I a:m really
worried." (line 10). PiC acknowledges N's attempt then hangs up
in line 13.

What could the negotiator have done differently? Our research
shows that explicit expressions of intention are not effective.
Such expressions lead either to stronger forms of resistance
from the person in crisis, or the person in crisis disengages with
the conversation-or worse, ends the conversation. Pushing for
their affiliation with good intentions is risky and rarely, if ever,
pays off. In other words, rapport (and trust) is not simply built by
claiming it. There is no short cut to achieving rapport, and, on
the way there are word choices that are risky. We have shown
how the persistence of highlighting and defining 'talk' and 'help'
as the central focus of negotiation is counter-productive for
engaging a PiC. In comparison, negotiators who use 'speak' and
'sort' to present their intentions face weaker forms of resistance
(Sikveland & Stokoe, 2020).

In Example 8.9, PiC has just been telling N about a problem he has had with a police officer. In line 01, N referring to this telling as a topic they "can talk about", is followed by a positive assessment, "That's good." (line 02).

```
Example 8.9: No need to talk about it
01   N:      >Okay well< we can talk about that Kevin,
02           That's good.=
03   N:      =[I'm glad– I'm glad you're starting to talk.=.hhhh]
04   PiC:    =[I've no need to talk about it,=I've just told you]
05           what he's doing,
```

Proposing to 'talk' (compared to proposals to 'speak') is regularly met by strong resistance in crisis negotiations. Putting a positive frame around the activity only serves to strengthen the resistance. Here, PiC makes explicit that he has got "no need to talk about it," (line 04), and hangs up soon after.

In Example 8.10, we see another case (from a different negotiation) of a negotiator putting a positive frame around "talking" (line 03): "talking costs nothing does it.". In the next turn, PiC rejects the proposal, with a disagreement, "Yeah it does,=It costs me time," (line 05).

```
Example 8.10: Talking costs nothing
01   N:      Let's just carry on talking for a while.
02                  (0.6)
03   N:      (cal-) talking costs nothing does it.
04                  (1.3)
05   PiC:    Yeah it does,=It costs me time,
06                  (0.6)
```

Earlier in this chapter, in Example 8.7, we argued that proposals to 'help' are counter-productive. Our research shows that people in crisis treat proposals to 'help' as unspecific -and therefore unhelpful. The problem with 'help' is that it is not tied to a specific action and is therefore easily challenged by PiC. In comparison, we find proposals to 'sort (out)' less vulnerable to explicit resistance or rejection. Example 8.11 is a case in point. PiC, now having turned 18, does not have the same access to social services, and the negotiator proposes that different mental health charities can provide support.

```
Example 8.11. We can sort that out
01  N:      Okay,=And also when we can sort out=.hh you know
02          if your mum's making up storie:s,.h then we
03          can sort that out.
04              (0.3)
05  N:      Okay?
06              (.)
07  PiC:   So if I go to the station what happens then.
```

Here, instead of rejecting N's proposals that they can find a solution regarding PiC's mother's behaviours, PiC invites N to elaborate how: "So if I go to the station what happens then." (line 07). This is a very different response to "you can't help me", which we find elsewhere, as N's proposals are already tied to something concrete that they can then work to elaborate.

In addition to 'help' and 'talk', another commonly used word to represent negotiators' good intentions is 'care'. Like explicit mentions of 'help' and 'talk', 'care' poses a persistent problem for negotiations, as people in crisis easily resist and see right through the façade of such terminology. Example 8.12 illustrates this point.

```
Example 8.12: Cos I care for you
01  N1:    What do you want me to call you.
02              (0.3)
```

```
03  PiC:    Why should I tell you my name yeah?
04  N1:     I told [you my na:me¿  ]
05  PiC:           [(that guy with)]
06          [who was- who was there (today).
07  N2:     [°Say (it's) cos I care for you°.
08               (.)
09  PiC:    [No.   ]
10  N2:     [°Cos I] care for you°.
11               (0.2)
12  N1:     I [care for you:?]
13  PiC:      [( )(coming)   ]  (down if I give) my  name.
14               (0.4)
15  N1:     If I didn't care for you I wouldn't be
16          [HERE. Would I.     ]
17  PiC:    [Why do you want to] get my NAME!
18               (0.3)
19  N1:     You're not <LISTENING TO ME:>.
```

This negotiation has come to a difficult stage, where PiC refuses to provide his name, and the primary negotiator (N1) keeps pushing for it. The secondary negotiator (N2) attempts to resolve the conflict by offering a candidate next turn: "say it's cos I care for you" (lines 07 and 10), which N1 eventually embeds into the conversation in line 12. We found that not only is the insistence on 'care' counter-productive, it is also an inappropriate N2 intervention at this stage (see Chapter 7). The escalated conflict continues, and little is achieved in terms of building or maintaining a positive relationship. We found that rapport, trust, and commitment is best built and preserved by (i) pursuing questions in the person in crisis's *own* domain of knowledge, and (ii) by trusting the person in crisis's *own* ability to make rational choices.

We have also explored the notions of emotion and empathy in our research. Being empathetic, understanding another's point of view, and reassuring an emotional person are important skills for working with a person in crisis. However, we find that naming and validating positive behaviour, and labelling emotions, can be risky. As Oostinga, Giebels and Taylor (2018, p. 21) suggest, "I understand how you feel" in crisis encounters is often counter-productive, and a person in crisis can easily reject this claim. In our data, we find very few examples of "you sound [sad, angry, upset]" or other formats that are typically used as examples of emotional labelling in the training literature. We found this interesting and have some suggestions to why this may be the case.

First, when working with an emotional person in crisis, it is best to accept their emotion and have them focus on the matters at hand. In the emergency call data, we found that call takers manage a emotions by giving the person in crisis a task and remaining persistent in accomplishing the task. Example 8.13 shows that when the caller shifts her focus to the person in need of help (line 03), the dispatcher (DIS) needs to redirect her attention to the task, getting the exact location so they can send help. In lines 01–02, the first request for the address goes unanswered as the caller turns to her father. By repeating, "Wha:t is the address", with added stress on "is" and "ad:dress", DIS is successful in shifting the caller's focus to the main task, and she responds immediately with her address (line 05).

```
Example 8.13: Dad Overdose
01   DIS:    Wha:t's thee
02           ad[dress.
03   CLR:       [OH MY GOD My dad's on th' mm-
04   DIS:    Wha:t [is the ad:dress.
05   CLR:          [↑Forty one↓ Go:pher Street.
```

In face-to-face situations, negotiators successfully handle a person in crisis's emotion without naming and validating emotions with phrases like, "you sound X". When we do find such cases, as in Example 8.14 where N1 labels the emotion, PiC resists the labelling.

```
Example 8.14: I'm not upset
01   N1:      Why are you upset.
02                  (8.1)
03   N1:      What are you upset about.
04                  (1.1)
05   PiC:     I'm not upset with a-  (.)
06            upset with anybody.
07                  (0.2)
08   PiC      They're upset with me.
09                  (0.2)
10   N1:      All right,
11                  (.)
12   N1:      <But I can see you're a bit
13            upset though.=i- What's
14            what's bothering you the most.
15                  (2.8)
16   N2:      ((clears throat)) °Why are they upset
              with you,°
```

Here, N1 asks a question in lines 01 and 03, that presumes PiC is upset: "Why are you upset." However, PiC denies this in line 05, "I'm not upset with a– (.) upset with anybody.". N1 nevertheless pursues the emotion based on what they claim to see (lines 12–14), before N2 suggests to N1 that they should reverse the object of PiC's 'upset': and ask, "Why are they upset with you," (line 16). PiC does not accept "upset" as a relevant category of emotion in this case.

Labelling emotions is risky: what gives someone the right to assume knowledge of another's emotions? One method for managing emotion in crisis encounters is to acknowledge the trouble as the person in crisis's domain whilst specifying a way forward. We see a clear case of that working in Example 8.15. The negotiators speak to PiC on the telephone. PiC is barricaded in his flat and is audibly crying throughout this conversation (represented by the ~ symbols in PiC's turns).

Example 8.15: You must have been so frightened
```
01   PiC:    ~.NHhhhh have you any idea.~
02                (.)
03   PiC:    ~(Ey) ( ) you ain't- you ain't
04           got a clue have ya.~
05                (0.3)
06   PiC:    ~.Hh[h you] know?~
07   N:         [.hh- ]
08                (0.2)
09   N:      [Simon ] I can hear it in your voice how:
10   PiC:    [~.MHHH~]
11   N:      [how dis]tressed that made you.=
12   PiC:    [~.MHHH~]
13   N:      How upset: (0.2) angry.=You- you- you
14           m- you must have
15           been so frightened.
16                (0.3)
17   PiC:    ~.MHHHH~
18                (0.2)
19   N:      [You must have been] so frightened.
20   PiC:    [~HHhhhh~           ]
21                (0.4)
22   PiC:    ~You have no idea miss seriously.~
23                (0.8)
24   N:      That's why I wanna t- I wanna-
25           I wanna come and sort this
26           out.=I wanna [talk to] you about it.=
27   PiC:                 [~.MHHH~]
28   N:      =And I've- promise you..hhhh it's me::?
29           (.) coming to talk >to you<.=That's
30           why I've given you this pri:vate pho:ne,
31           (.) so it's you and me. (0.5) and we
```

```
32              can get this sorted out.
33                      (2.1)
34   PiC:    Okay.
35   N:      [Is that] alri[:ght.]
36   PiC:    [(yes-) ]        [Yes ] that'd be nice.
```

In line 09, N says what she can hear in PiC's voice, reporting
a past feeling when PiC had attempted suicide. With, "You
must have been so frightened" (lines 14–15 and 19), N then
topicalizes the emotion and gives PiC something to talk about.
In response, PiC denies N's full access to his emotions while
also admitting that the emotional labels matched, "~You have
no idea miss seriously.~" (line 22). N, without claiming to fully
understand PiC's emotions, now has a clear path for supporting
PiC and resolving the crisis. In lines 24–32, N proposes why
she wants to talk with PiC, which PiC accepts in lines 34/36.
Thus, N here manages to use PiC's emotions to propose a way
forward. Labelling emotions alone does not build a positive
relationship.

'Mirroring' is, like 'labelling emotions', one of the features
representing active listening skills in the training literature,
but of which we find few examples in our data. One form
of doing 'mirroring' is to repeat, in confirmation, what the
interlocutor has just said. Such repetition may support shared
understanding, or agreement, and further progress of the
encounter. But sometimes – and here lies the risk involved
with mirroring – repeating what a person has just said may
be treated as not hearing or challenging them. Example 8.16
demonstrates this point (this example is taken from a suicide
helpline, in a conference paper by DiDomenico, 2018; used with
kind permission).

```
Example 8.16: Why are you repeating everything I say
39   CT:     How long have you felt like this.
40                   (1.1)
41   CLR:    It's been going on this year for a whi:le.
```

```
42                    (1.1)
43   CT:    Mm hm.
44                    (4.2)
45   CLR:   It's har:d though.
46                    (1.2)
49   CT:    It's hard,
50   CLR:   >It's very hard.<
51                    (3.8)
52   CT:    Mm
53                    (2.8)
53   CLR:   I don't think my medicine is working,
54                    (1.0)
55   CT:    You don't think your medicine is working?
56                    (0.2)
57   CLR:   Why are you repeating everything I say.
```

The call taker (CT) works to unpack the caller's (CLR) distress, giving them a chance to talk (line 39), and after the silence at line 40, the caller begins their narrative, "it's been going on this year for a whi:le" (line 40). The caller's turn projects a longer turn, and the call taker remains silent in favour of waiting for the caller to continue (line 42, continuer at 43, and line 44). When the caller speaks next they say, "It's har:d though." (line 45) casting their trouble as difficult, giving the call taker an opportunity to ask more about why, or what the caller feels is so challenging. However, after a long silence at line 46, and in the place where the call taker could advance the call, they produce a partial repeat of the caller's prior turn, "It's hard," (line 49), ending with a rising intonation which invites the caller to say more. We find however, the caller does not treat the repeat with rising intonation as an invitation to open up. Rather, they upgrade their trouble talk, ">It's very hard.<" (line 50), again giving the call taker an opportunity to unpack the caller's trouble. In the same call, we find the call taker uses repetition once more, but this time repeating the caller's complaint, "I don't think my medicine is working," (line 53), which the caller repeats in its entirety, with a rising intonation at line 55. Conversation analytic research has shown that full-verbatim rising repeats such as this signals trouble with the action of the prior speaker's turn, calling the it into question by treating it out of place (Robinson & Kevoe-Feldman, 2010). In this case, however, the caller treats the call taker's action of repeating each question as problematic by complaining about the technique at line 57, "Why are you repeating everything I say."

In line with the lessons we show throughout this book, sometimes training techniques that make sense in simulation exercise do not work in the same way in practice. Mirroring actions is one of those techniques that 1) is rarely used in practice and 2) has the potential to create moments of misalignment between the crisis professional and PiC.

FROM PRACTICE TO TRAINING: CHOOSING THE RIGHT WORDS, AND WHAT IT REALLY MEANS TO BUILD RAPPORT

1. Building relationships (trust and rapport) is not achieved by claiming to be genuine. It is achieved by *showing* you are genuine. Negotiators who keep asking and pursuing questions in a person in crisis's domain are in a better position to achieve rapport than those who insist that they "care".

2. Propose to 'speak' to a person in crisis, not 'talk'. Proposals to 'talk' are easier to reject than proposals to 'speak'. This is because 'talking' has a closer relationship with (positive or negative) evaluations of dialogue than 'speaking' (see Sikveland & Stokoe, 2020). A person in crisis can say, "I don't want to *talk*", but does not say, "I don't want to *speak*".

3. Propose to 'sort out' (and how), not 'help'. 'Helping' is a less concrete action than 'sorting', making that proposal more vulnerable to resistance based on its unspecificity and irrelevance.

4. Emotional labelling is risky. Successful call takers in emergency calls may acknowledge emotions but (re-)focus on practical matters at hand to resolve the crisis. Successful negotiators make sure the emotions are actually evident before

making reference to them; and they use emotions as a reason to support a person in crisis, not as an exercise in its own right.

5. Repeating a person in crisis's words ('mirroring') is risky. Repetition can be heard as a problem in hearing or a challenge and is not evident as productive for how crisis negotiations are managed in our data.

Further reading in this book

We have shown how some words are easier to resist or reject than others (Chapter 3); how crisis professionals manage strong emotions (Chapter 4), and how interventions from secondary negotiators do not always fit the unfolding conversation with the person in crisis (Chapter 7).

SCAFFOLDING A RESOLUTION: HOW TO SUPPORT THE AGENDA OF THE PERSON IN CRISIS

At the core of what makes negotiations work effectively is the ability to shift focus onto the other party: and enable them to make their own decisions on their own behalf. How do negotiators make this possible? Our research illustrates the scaffolding work negotiators do, not to force the person in crisis to move to safety but to set up the right conditions for deciding to do so. This takes time and patience.

Existing training often highlights how negotiators should avoid being confrontational by challenging, arguing, or yelling. But, as with all forms of social action, one should exercise caution defining 'confrontation' and 'arguing' in advance or dismissing them as counter-productive. Indeed, some forms of confrontation, or challenge, are necessary to achieve resolution or to enact the 'problem solving' phase of the negotiation cycle (Ireland & Vecchi, 2009). Our research shows how some challenges work to move the negotiation productively forwards, or to demonstrate commitment.

Below, removed from interactional context, we list phrases that negotiators actually used and which proved to be productive in moving the negotiation forward:

- "Why don't you go and sit on another bit"
- "Don't ignore me"

- "I'm starting to get a bit fed up now"
- "Why are you laughing?"
- "Well then answer me"
- "Well if it doesn't make a difference, take it off then"
- "I have to stand here, *with* you"
- "You're gonna have to hold *me*"
- "Are you scared of heights? Obviously not cos you're up there!"

We will leave it up to the reader to judge whether they find it surprising that these utterances, all produced by negotiators, were key components of positive turning points in crisis negotiations. It is worth noting, however, that none of these phrases resemble problem-solving examples found in the training literature. In this final section of this chapter, we demonstrate the relevance of some of the utterances listed above (the remaining ones are handled in Chapter 5 and 6 of the book), regarding how negotiators *scaffold a positive resolution* to the crisis.

First, Example 8.16 shows how a negotiator challenges PiC on the fact that he sits on one side of the roof, while he just as well could sit on another bit (the former represents a more precarious side of the roof than the latter, but this is not said in so many words to PiC). The PiC decides to move to the safer part of the roof.

```
Example 8.17: Sit on another bit
01   N1:    You've got all control over there,
02          That whole roof is yours.
03              (.)
04   N1:    We're not coming up there, (.) so why do
05          you got to sit on that bit.
06              (6.6)
07   N1:    Why don't you go and sit (.) on another bit.
08              (3.6)
09   N1:    Sit at the other end.=Where you can
            speak to
```

From practice to training

```
10              (d-) (0.2) Kathy.
11                    (0.5)
12   N2:    °Y:es:::°
```

The negotiator (N1) appeals to PiC's agency and control in
lines 01–02: "You've got all control over there, That whole roof
is yours." Perhaps more importantly, N1 appeals to *PiC's own
ability/willingness to make rational decisions.* N1 proceeds
to scaffold such a rational decision by claiming they will not
act against their promises, like coming up to grab PiC ("We're
not coming up there,", line 04), implying that there is nothing
that prevents PiC from moving to safety. After a long gap (line
06), N1 pursues the proposal, "Why don't you go and sit (.) on
another bit.", before specifying a location where Kathy (another
negotiator that PiC has engaged with earlier) is positioned.
Around line 11, PiC starts moving, and we can see N2 reacting to
this in line 12.

Example 8.17 is taken from a couple of hours into the
negotiation. Several features suggest that there has already been
some progress in terms of relationship building. By comparison,
Example 8.18 shows how the negotiator makes similar appeals to
PiC's agency and control during early stages of the same crisis
encounter. Here, N1 is unsuccessful in getting PiC to comply.

```
Example 8.18: You can come down
01   N1:    But you can stop this. Can't you.
02   PiC:   No.=
03   N1:    =You're- you can stop this:.
04                   (0.2)
05   N1:    You are comple:tely in contro:l.
06                   (0.3)
07 N1:    You can stop this.=You can come do:wn.
08                   (2.2)
09   PiC:   No.
10                   (0.2)
11   PiC:   I'm not coming down.
```

12   (6.5)

13   PiC: I hope you get paid good overtime.

In lines 03 and 05, N1 appeals to PiC's agency and control, quite explicitly with "You are comple:tely in contro:l." (line 05). There is no immediate answer, then N1 moves on to propose that (as a consequence) PiC "can come do:wn." (line 07). The PiC rejects this proposal in line 09, before expanding ("I'm not coming down.", line 11), undermining the negotiator's efforts ("I hope you get paid good overtime.", line 13). Thus, framing reasoning on PiC's own control does not work in and by itself. There is further scaffolding work required for influence to happen, and to appeal to PiC's willingness to make rational decisions.

Example 8.18, compared to Example 8.17, exposes the problem of not creating enough scaffolding to warrant agreement to the proposal ('come down'). By complying early, PiC would, in effect, completely change his stance and appear irrational. This is key to understanding how negotiators avoid 'moving too fast too soon', and how crisis negotiations work. A person in crisis will not agree to 'come down' but will, however (in most cases), come down safely. Successful negotiators understand the scaffolding work it takes to achieve progress.

Successful negotiators are also 'committed' and 'consistent' (see McMains & Mullins, 2014). What does commitment look like in practice? With our final example, we show how a negotiator, faced with strong attempts at undermining her commitment to PiC's wellbeing, rejects PiC's challenge and appeals in no uncertain terms to PiC's ability to understand the point she is making.

Example 8.19: You know how it works
01   PiC: Bloody- (0.2) you can just fucking go
02   back to your station.=
03   N1:   =No I CA:N't. How can I do that.
04   You know how it works, I can't do that.
05   Can I. I have to sta:nd he:re, (0.4) With you.

```
06                    (3.1)
07    N1:    But you're telling me you're not trying to
08           piss me o:ff.
09                    (7.1)
10    N1:    It feels like you are¿ It feels like you
11           just want to upset me.
12                    (3.2)
13    N1:    Will you come do:wn.
14                    (1.5)
15    N2:    Watch your step mate,
16                    (0.3)
17    N2:    Watch your step.
```

The turns in focus are lines 03–05. What the negotiator does here may seem risky but is highly effective. First, she rejects PiC's attempt at undermining her commitment outright ("No I CA:N't"). Importantly, N does not leave the apparent "arguing" at that. N challenges PiC in the form of a question: "How can I do that." This is not a question for PiC to answer. However, it emerges as a rhetorical question; N answers it herself. The challenge proceeds by a direct appeal to PiC's ability to understand her logic, "You know how it works," (line 04), and finally "I have to sta:nd he:re, (0.4) With you." (line 05). This final sentence could resemble a complaint. However, in this context, it works to support N's strong argument, in favour of her commitment to a resolution of the crisis. Soon after, PiC moves towards safety: he moves safely down from the roof he has been on for about three hours since the negotiation started.

FROM PRACTICE TO TRAINING: HOW NEGOTIATORS SCAFFOLD A RESOLUTION TO THE CRISIS

1. Persons in crisis do not *agree* to 'come down'. Successful negotiators set up conditions for persons in crisis to choose safety over harm. This works over extended sequences of talk, through which the negotiator appeals to the person in crisis's ability to make rational decisions.

2. 'Arguing', 'confrontations', and 'challenges' are not necessarily problematic or risky for the negotiation. Successful negotiators leverage logic/reasoning and trust the person in crisis's ability to do the same.

Further reading in this book

We have shown how crisis negotiators overcome resistance by leveraging logic grounded in and displayed through the words of the person in crisis (Chapter 5), and how negotiators scaffold their decisions to choose safety over harm (Chapter 6).

SUMMARY: CHALLENGES FOR FUTURE RESEARCH AND TRAINING

When it comes to a conversation as important as negotiating with a person in suicidal crisis, we are presented with a situation in which it is easy – and crucial – to see that every turn matters. Key to any successful negotiation is getting the person in crisis to take turns. Every time they say something, they are choosing to stay alive. Every single time. In much of the negotiation literature, the outcome of situations like these, when someone is threatening harm to themselves, are understood in terms of the factors and variables of psychology – it will depend on the person's intentions, attitudes, mental and physical health history, and so on. While these are all important, when a police negotiator arrives at a scene, they often do not know anything about the person they are about to have a conversation with. Their only tool is the interaction itself. What is more, because we generally think that people either 'really' intend to take their own life or do not, we might not accept that language can constrain and afford what happens. And so we do not study what really happens, and therefore remain unaware at any explicit level of what is effective.

The negotiator's core communication skills – such as active listening – when listed as categories of interaction, have remained underspecified until now. Our conversation analytic research has enabled the presentation of numerous cases of actual negotiation, in precise detail. We have been able to see the turns taken by negotiators that solve the problems presented by persons in crisis in every turn, displaying their experience and expertise for us to describe. Our recordings are of negotiation *in the wild*, as it happens, not recorded for research purposes at all, but providing data for a naturally occurring experiment, in which we can see what happens in response to a particular way negotiators ask persons in crisis to engage in the process, or in response to offers of support, or help, or care. Treating Active Listening Skills as a box-ticking exercise runs the risk of not capturing when and how precise empirical realizations of them are relevant and productive for the interaction, in context.

Many of our findings have challenged existing training, and even the mottos and straplines of negotiator practice (for example, NYPD's "talk to me"). However, we are not challenging negotiation practice; rather, we are illuminating practice in a way that we hope is enabling. For instance, we showed that words really matter – asking a person in crisis to 'speak' is more productive for the negotiation than asking them to 'talk'. Asking questions – something which may be caricatured as too 'pushy' or imposition on the person in crisis – is in fact core to a successful outcome. We found that questions, especially when used to show interest in the person in crisis and elicit their story, their decisions, and their agency, are central resources that negotiation training should embrace.

While much of the crisis negotiation literature and training focuses on hostage situations, the most common type of job is suicidal crisis. For our police partners, this was often the first time they had focused on the most common, but perhaps less newsworthy and headline-grabbing, part of their daily work. A large number of recommendations in various negotiation training manuals remain untested and are more than we have been able to evaluate in our research so far. There is much to be done. In addition to suicide threats, many crisis negotiators work across hostage and terrorism incidents, where there is – from our perspective – a similar under-specification of practice in terms of its precise turn-by-turn composition.

We have shown that words matter. Negotiators open up and close down opportunities to the person in crisis to resist the negotiation through the words they select to generate and progress the negotiation. If we examine what happens in conversation, we learn the power of words to change outcomes – including in situations of life and death.

REFERENCES

Di Domenico, S. (2018, July). *Inviting elaboration or initiating repair? Use of rising-intoned repetition in the environment of initiating actions as professional technique on a crisis help line.* Conference paper: International Society for Conversation Analysis, Loughborough, UK.

Ireland, C. A., & Vecchi, G. M. (2009). The Behavioral Influence Stairway Model (BISM): a framework for managing terrorist crisis situations? *Behavioral Sciences of Terrorism and Political Aggression, 1*(3), 203–218.

McMains, M., & W. Mullins. 2014. *Crisis negotiations: Managing critical incidents and hostage situations in law enforcement and corrections.* New York: Routledge.

Miller, L. (2005). Hostage negotiation: Psychological principles and practices. *International Journal of Emergency Mental Health, 7*(4), 277.

Mullins, W. C. (2002). Advanced communication techniques for hostage negotiators. *Journal of Police Crisis Negotiations, 2*(1), 63–81.

Oostinga, M. S., Giebels, E., & Taylor, P. J. (2018). 'An error is feedback': the experience of communication error management in crisis negotiations. *Police Practice and Research, 19*(1), 17–30.

Robinson, J. D., & Kevoe-Feldman, H. (2010). Using full repeats to initiate repair on others' questions. *Research on Language and Social Interaction, 43*(3), 232–259.

Sikveland, R. O., Kevoe-Feldman, H., & Stokoe, E. (2020). Overcoming suicidal persons' resistance using productive communicative challenges during police crisis negotiations. *Applied Linguistics, 41*(4), 533–551.

Stokoe, E. (2014). The Conversation Analytic Role-play Method (CARM): A method for training communication skills as an alternative to simulated role-play. *Research on Language and Social Interaction, 47*(3), 255–265.

Stokoe, E., & Sikveland, R. O. (2017). The conversation analytic role-play method. In Pink, S. Fors, V. & O'Dell, T. *Theoretical scholarship and applied practice*, Vol. 11 (pp. 73–96). Berghahn Books.

Stokoe, E., & Sikveland, R. O. (2020). The backstage work negotiators do when communicating with persons in crisis. *Journal of Sociolinguistics, 24*(2), 185–208.

Stokoe, E., Humă, B., Sikveland, R. O., & Kevoe-Feldman, H. (2020). When delayed responses are productive: Being persuaded following resistance in conversation. *Journal of Pragmatics, 155*, 70–82.

Van Hasselt, V. B., Romano, S. J., & Vecchi, G. M. (2008). Role playing: Applications in hostage and crisis negotiation skills training. *Behavior Modification, 32*(2), 248–263.

Vecchi, G.M., Van Hasselt, V.B., & Romano, S.S. (2005). Crisis (hostage) negotiation: Current strategies and issues in high-risk conflict resolution, *Aggression and Violent Behaviour, 10*, 533–551.

Index